W9-DBF-606

COMMITTE
TEAMS

COMMITTED TEAMS

Three Steps to Inspiring Passion and Performance

MARIO MOUSSA, MADELINE BOYER, AND DEREK NEWBERRY

With Contributions from
Joanne Baron
Vishal Bhatia
Amy Brown
Lauren Hirshon
Michael Joiner
Annette Mattei
Renée Gillespie Torchia

WILEY

Published by John Wiley & Sons, Inc., Hoboken, New Jersey.
Published simultaneously in Canada.

For general information about our other products and services, please contact our Customer Care
Department within the United States at (800) 762-2974, outside the United States at (317)
572-3993, or fax (317) 572-4002.

Wiley publishes in a variety of print and electronic formats and by print-on-demand. Some material
included with standard print versions of this book may not be included in e-books or in
print-on-demand. If this book refers to media such as a CD or DVD that is not included in the
version you purchased, you may download this material at http://booksupport.wiley.com. For more
information about Wiley products, visit www.wiley.com.

Library of Congress Cataloging-in-Publication Data:

Names: Moussa, Mario, author. | Boyer, Madeline, 1987- author. | Newberry,
    Derek, 1983- author.
Title: Committed teams : three steps to inspiring passion and performance /
    Mario Moussa, Madeline Boyer, Derek Newberry.
Description: Hoboken : Wiley, 2016. | Includes bibliographical references and
    index.
Identifiers: LCCN 2015042388 (print) | LCCN 2015047335 (ebook) | ISBN
    9781119157403 (hardback) | ISBN 9781119157410 (pdf) | ISBN 9781119157427
    (epub)
Subjects: LCSH: Teams in the workplace–Management. | Employee motivation. |
    Leadership. | BISAC: BUSINESS & ECONOMICS / Workplace Culture.
Classification: LCC HD66 .M68 2016 (print) | LCC HD66 (ebook) | DDC
    658.4/022–dc23
LC record available at http://lccn.loc.gov/2015042388

Cover Design: Wiley
Cover Image: © iStock.com/furtaev
Illustrations by: Barbara Boyer

Printed in the United States of America

10 9 8 7 6 5 4 3 2 1

For Robin Komita
—Mario Moussa

For Robert and Ana Boyer
—Madeline Boyer

For Carolyn Newberry
—Derek Newberry

CONTENTS

7 Who Has a Good Idea? Insights on Innovation

8 Lead or Follow? Guidelines for Leadership Groups

9 Why Are We Here? Engaging Committees

PREFACE

Our teamwork philosophy is easy to describe. You get organized, schedule regular times to check on your progress, and make adjustments when necessary. Three steps.

Simple.

The hard part is actually following the steps during your typical workday: time-crunched and stressful, deadline-driven, often chaotic, and full of quirky characters who have surprising motives. Not so simple—but that is a common reality. We wrote this book for teams who have to deliver results under these difficult conditions. Though it originated in the research we conducted at the Wharton School of Business, we organized our findings in the form of a how-to guide.

In Part One, we describe the three-step process for creating and maintaining a *committed team*. The process begins with establishing the three foundations of successful teamwork: goals, roles, and norms. Combine the three foundations with the three steps, and you have what we call the 3x3 Framework—or the 3x3, for short. We recommend you read Part One from beginning to end, so that you understand the whole 3x3 and how to apply it. Each chapter includes a tool that you can start using right away.

Part Two is about five common types of teaming: virtual teams, startups, innovation projects, leadership groups, and committees. If you are especially interested in learning how to manage a particular type of teamwork, you can go right to the chapter about it in this part after reading about the basic 3x3. Of course, you are welcome to read straight through Part Two, and we hope you will after finishing Part One. Each chapter in the second half of the book offers lessons you will find valuable no matter what your team needs to accomplish.

The three of us collaborated with a group of contributing authors who are experts in social science and organizational consulting. You can read about their backgrounds in the Authors section.

We tell lots of teamwork stories that we have heard over the years. We are interested in hearing your story, too. Please get in touch with us at www.committedteams.com

—Mario Moussa, Madeline Boyer, and Derek Newberry

INTRODUCTION
"CAN I MAKE MY TEAM WORK?"

Intense!

Twisting your features into a mask of pain, you dig your heels into the soft grass. A rope tears into your palms. Sweat runs down your face as blood seeps from spidery cracks in your skin and onlookers gawk and yell.

A clear, tiny voice speaks to you amid the cacophony of confused thoughts swirling in your head: "So-o-o-o … what am I learning from this experience?"

Well, you should be learning about teamwork. You are in the middle of a typical organizational development exercise. This one happens to entail pulling a large rock 30 feet. Your supervisor decided to start by having you try going it alone. Yet, despite all of your 5 A.M. Crossfit workouts at the gym, you failed to move the boulder even an inch. To achieve a different result, you clearly need to work with others.

Teamwork gets things done, right?

As others join you, one by one, the collective rope-pulling effort seems to demonstrate the point. Little by little, the boulder starts moving until it nudges over the 30-foot mark. Cheers erupt. But you notice something odd. With each additional person who contributes to the effort, the boulder moves a little bit faster, but not as fast as you would have imagined. By the time the tenth person steps up, you feel the group is barely pulling harder than when it was only six, even though everyone seems to be working hard.

Afterward, you ask others if they noticed the same thing. Everyone says: "*I* was pulling my weight, but it sure seems that others weren't."

1 + 1 = … 1.5? If the boulder exercise sounds like something you have experienced on your own team, then you have encountered a well-known phenomenon first identified by Max Ringelmann in the early twentieth century: social loafing.[1] It names the tendency to apply less and less effort to a task as more people become involved with it.

In the original studies of what became known as the Ringelmann Effect, the French engineer analyzed the amount of energy expended by his students in a rope-pulling contest. As each side expanded its team, each person became less committed to the task, subconsciously slacking off more and more. No synergies here: 1 + 1 equals something less than 2, as illustrated in Figure I.1. This is just one in a long list of bad habits that most teams tend to cultivate over time, even though they might not be aware of it.

Teamwork Everywhere, All the Time

Flawed or not, teams show no signs of going away. Increasingly, in fact, being good at teamwork is synonymous with simply being good at work. And for a valid reason: the complexity of today's world—shaped by rapidly accelerating technological, economic, and cultural trends—demands that organizations of all kinds seek out the

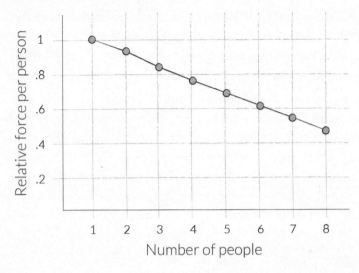

Figure I.1   Effects of Social Loafing on People Pulling on a Rope

synergistic potential of teams. But too often what teams deliver is a lot of talk and little accountability. How many team kickoff meetings have left you, just a few minutes afterward, not quite sure of what the heck was accomplished? And wait—when is the next meeting, anyway?

Hence the basic question that led us to write this book: How do you create a team that is committed to high performance when few teams end up being truly greater than the sum of their parts? Our answer is a simple framework: the 3x3. It is built on three foundations and supports an interactive three-step process. By helping you get better at leading teams, the 3x3 will help you get better at virtually all aspects of your work.

A Teamwork Laboratory: Creating the 3x3 Framework

Our own team came together through the Executive Development Program (EDP) at the Wharton School of Business. We were a group of assorted organizational specialists—social scientists, MBAs, and management consultants—with decades of combined experience researching and solving problems related to group dynamics. Mario

Moussa, co-director of Wharton's Strategic Persuasion Workshop and an EDP faculty member, gave us one goal: produce a field-tested process for creating and leading High-Performing Teams (HPTs).

Wharton's EDP, an immersive two-week experience, attracts leaders and rising stars who come from all around the world to develop a broad range of business skills. Participants learn under the guidance of top faculty and Academic Director Peter Fader, the Frances and Pei-Yuan Chia Professor of Marketing. One of the core components of the program is a highly realistic business simulation that creates a living teamwork laboratory. Because EDP participants are the best of the best, the program is an ideal environment in which to stress-test our theories about what makes teams tick and how they get better.

To give you a sense of how this "laboratory" works and why it helps crystallize the key features of high- and low-performing teams, let us bring you into the world of the simulation, entering the way hundreds of participants do every year. At the beginning, you sit huddled in a conference room with six other executives from nearly every continent on the planet. They are your teammates. But you have never met any of them before and, given the number of languages spoken in the room, you may have trouble communicating with them about even the most basic topics.

To make matters worse, you know next to nothing about your company's industry, and neither does anyone else, because it is organized around medical devices that don't exist in the real world. Nevertheless, all of you have to quickly ramp up and, as a team, make a series of business decisions. Biggest issue: Sales are down in your company's most important region. Why? Is it product quality? Poor marketing? Your team needs to do research into the possible causes before it can determine what to do and where to invest. Your peers will scrutinize your team's decisions and results in a public forum.

Do you want to join this company? Probably not, because it sounds like a nightmare. But we would strongly encourage you to spend a few days of your life working in it. You would learn a lot there. We certainly have.

In this setting, we took on the challenge of creating a process that any team can use to boost engagement and continually improve performance, no matter how diverse the group, or how unwieldy its challenges. We knew that if the approach we created worked in the chaotic world of the EDP simulation, it could work anywhere. So far, we have observed, analyzed, and supported the development of more than 100 of these EDP teams. With each running of the program, we have assessed and made adjustments to our team-building framework. Combining our insights from the simulation with our own individual experiences as researchers and consultants, we created the 3x3 Framework for producing team results that are greater than the sum of individual members' efforts.

Step One: Commit
Establish Commitments
Step Two: Check
Check Alignment
Step Three: Close
Close the Saying-Doing Gap

The first 3 stands for the Three Foundations of HPTs: clear goals, roles, and norms. If you have read or heard anything about good teamwork, you are probably familiar with some version of these foundations. We bet you have also felt frustrated in trying to establish them. Even with the best of intentions, teammates quickly stray from commitments. At times, getting everyone on the same page can feel like endlessly translating your thoughts into a language you barely understand and communicating with a group of people from strange and unfamiliar cultures—such as finance, IT, sales, and manufacturing. Research shows that, in the workplace, these internal subcultures matter at least as much as national ones and cause just as many communication headaches. You collaborate across these functional cultures many times a day, and often through emails and conference calls. The key to getting the most out of your team is to understand this boundary-crossing and why it often seems like the work of getting aligned is always just out of your grasp.

To address the issue of alignment, we created a three-step process for resolving differences and deepening commitment. We call the three steps Commit, Check, and Close. The steps may seem simple—because they are. Which is the whole point: complicated flow charts and high-level mantras are not going to help you ignite passion and improve your team's performance in the real world of work. The three-step process will help keep your teammates on track and stay committed to their goals, roles, and norms. In this sense, HPTs play by the rules: the commitments they make to the Three Foundations.

High-Performing Teams Play by the Rules—But Which Ones?

Stop us if you've heard this joke before.

Two young fish are swimming along and they happen to meet an older fish swimming the other way. The older one nods and says, "Morning, boys. How's the water?" The two young fish keep going and eventually one of them looks over at the other and asks, "What the heck is water?"

This particular version of the joke is adapted from a college graduation speech given by the late novelist David Foster Wallace.[2] But the challenge he illustrates is a universal one. The hardest things to notice are often right in front of our faces—things like our own and others' thoughts and feelings, and also the implicit rules that govern how we interact with others. Virtually all teams underperform because of this disconnect between psychological awareness and the reality of a group's social environment.

We call this phenomenon the illusion of insight—insight into the motivations that produce our actions. What we think we know about others and ourselves is, more often than not, surprisingly misguided. But we jump to conclusions anyway.

Decades of psychological research reveal that we believe we know our own minds far better than we actually do, and it also turns out that we have as much difficulty knowing others' thoughts as we do understanding our own. Psychologist Nicholas Epley describes a famous experiment in which couples were asked to answer a series of questions about each other's preferences, and then guess how accurate they were.[3] The participants were right about 30 percent of the time, but they guessed they had been right about 80 percent of the time. In other words, they were shockingly overconfident about how well they knew each other—and these were couples in long-term relationships. Imagine how much tougher it can be to understand co-workers.

The bottom line: we often think we understand ourselves and our team even as we miscommunicate and misinterpret intentions, over-estimate our ability to perform a task, and fail to recognize our own assumptions about the way work should be done. Every team needs clear rules. The trick is to make the rules explicit so that everybody understands what they are and remains committed to them.

Teamwork Rules = Culture

We human beings are wired to create rules that enable us to live and work together. These rules help solve problems big and small, such as: "How do we build a fire to keep from freezing?" or "Where should we go out for dinner tonight?" or "How are we going to get this project done on time and on budget?" In short, such rules govern collective behavior. Many social scientists claim that the ability to create and follow collective problem-solving rules is a defining human characteristic. Because all of us have this ability, we co-exist harmoniously—most of the time anyway—in tribes, villages, cities, and countries. Furthermore, in work-related settings, we are able to collaborate in teams and organizations.

A long line of anthropologists defines these problem-solving rules as "culture," which groups express through language, symbols, and behaviors. Put two or more people together and a culture starts to take shape automatically. As the venerable social theorist Clifford Geertz observed, culture is what defines humans as social beings. Without it, attempts to collaborate would degenerate into *a mere chaos of pointless acts and exploding emotions.*"[4]

> Culture has many definitions used for many purposes.
>
> The dictionary says culture is "the attitudes and behavior characteristics of a particular social group."
>
> Lou Gerstner of IBM said, "Culture isn't just one aspect of the game. It is the game."
>
> Our research reveals:
> *Culture = Rules for Solving Problems*

Long story short: human beings need culture to get along, and your team needs its own culture to get work done.

Therefore, the first step in creating a high-performing team is establishing its culture. In the most practical sense, culture is the set of rules—or commitments—that govern how you work together with your teammates to solve problems. A shared culture helps teams adapt and thrive in challenging environments in both the natural and the business worlds. But culture causes problems, too. We often misinterpret our own group's rules for collaborating and are blind to ingrained behaviors that actually undermine performance.

Thus, a puzzle: Why is culture both the most important aspect of team success and the biggest barrier to it? Answer: familiarity equals invisibility.

Try a small thought experiment: Imagine you and a friend have stepped onto a crowded elevator in a tall building as your workday is starting. As people rush on, one person stands directly in front of the buttons. After a few "Ahem"s and "Excuse me"s, this person moves away from the buttons, squeezing right between you and your friend and staring at the back of the elevator. The crowd eventually empties out, yet the stranger is still standing shoulder to shoulder with you, even though there is plenty of space to move away.

How would you describe this person's behavior? As "bizarre," of course. Imagine how we felt when we conducted this experiment—acting as the stranger—in an undergraduate anthropology class.

Now consider why this stranger's behavior seems so bizarre. Everyone knows you are supposed to face the front rather than the back of the elevator. You were probably told how to behave in this situation by a parent when you were little, or you simply watched others and learned through trial and error what you were supposed to do. And then, at a certain point, you stopped having to think about it. You just knew how and where to stand in an elevator without anyone telling you. The formal, explicit rules governing your behavior became informal and unspoken—even unconscious. This is how culture works.

As a group's rules accumulate over time, a culture forms in ways that can be largely invisible to team members, and individuals often begin operating by new rules that conflict with the team's explicit rules in ways they are not aware of.

Comprehensive and often contradictory, all of these rules just become "the way we do things around here." People may not even be aware of or remember why certain ways of doing things developed in the first place. Culture often works wonders and makes social life more efficient, as in the case of elevator-riding. But there is another side to the story, too. Imagine being on a startup team with a laid-back culture where everyone shows up to meetings 10 minutes late. This behavior might help boost morale and create group rapport at first, though it could become a major liability as the startup grows and the volume of work increases.

Becoming aware of your culture and managing it effectively is more than just a fun team building activity. *It is the key to your success.*

Make the Rules

Creating and leading a team affords a rare opportunity to consciously and deliberately cultivate a few key cultural rules for getting work done. Research on group dynamics shows that teams perform best when they agree on rules related to goals, roles, and norms—or what we call the Three Foundations. *Commit*, the first step in the process of creating an HPT, produces basic agreements about these foundations. (see Figure I.2).

1. Goals: Rules guiding the team's direction   Do you have a shared vision and specific goals that not only establish clear performance targets, but also tap into the *values* that are meaningful to individual members?

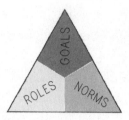

Figure I.2   The Three Foundations

2. Roles: Rules defining each member's contribution   Do you have clearly defined roles that include both the *formal* and *informal* aspects of teamwork, such as facilitation, coaching, and mediation?

3. Norms: Rules determining how members interact   Do you have mechanisms for making decisions, sharing information, and resolving conflicts so that clear expectations are set for team *behaviors*?

While rule-making is an essential first step, it is one that must be continually revisited. Team members inevitably create new rules that can undermine the original foundations of the team. This is why Steps Two and Three of the HPT process—*Check* and *Close*—involve checking on alignment with the original commitments and closing the gap between stated commitments and actual behaviors.

The Case of the Diamondbacks

As an example of how this process works, consider a team we observed in EDP: the Diamondbacks. The Diamondbacks were eight guys with big personalities who immediately clicked when they met and decided to form a team. Former soldiers and athletes, the Diamondbacks adopted the "Git-R-Done" motto. Made famous by the blue-collar comedian, Larry the Cable Guy, the catchphrase (and maybe philosophy of life) is all about just putting your head down and doing the job. In other words, for the Diamondbacks, speed and action—livened up with a heavy dose of locker room humor—were priorities over long-range planning.

They were an energetic group that meshed right away, and they established their culture up front. Git-R-Done guided the rules that would align this group of doers and propel them to dominance in the simulation—or so they thought. But by the middle of the first week, the Diamondbacks were struggling and their commitment to the team was flagging. Their turbo-charged culture had pushed them to make deal after deal. In fact, they did so well, they oversold. In the process, they incinerated relationships with other teams by failing to deliver on the sales they had promised. Their big personalities that helped to grease the wheels of making deals were suddenly viewed as political and untrustworthy.

Despite their Git-R-Done approach, the Diamondbacks unfortunately ended up getting little if anything done for the first half of the workshop. Their team observer helped them become aware of ways the rules they had created were out of sync with the environment of the sim. The team culture was dragging down performance. Drawing on the power of their brotherhood, however, the Diamonbacks pulled together during more than one come-to-Jesus moment. At the end of the two-week EDP, they were on an upward trajectory and in high spirits. In a word, they were committed. They are still one of the most legendary of EDP teams, a great example of the benefits and dangers of a strong culture and its rules.

The Diamondbacks saw firsthand that even when you make the rules and build consensus, team members can just as quickly fall out of alignment once they get into the flow of their day-to-day work. For this reason, we agree with group dynamics experts like the late Harvard professor J. Richard Hackman,[5] who has demonstrated that teams need to establish the right foundational factors like goals and roles to be successful. But we also have found that building these foundations—the first step in the HPT process—is not enough to ensure that a team consistently amounts to more than the sum of its parts. As we saw with the Diamondbacks, and as you have probably seen on your own teams, a disconnect between team commitments and team behaviors inevitably begins to appear.

Become Your Own Observer

Alignment is a stubborn problem, and its roots lie in the failure to regularly check in about commitments. The second step in the process—checking in—can be hard because of what we called the illusion of insight, which blinds your team to underlying conflicts. An outside observer can help you see these conflicts. On your own team, however, you may have to cultivate the ability to be your own observer. But this step takes more than pointing out shortcomings.

When you first address the fact that members are not fulfilling their commitments, chances are you will be met with denial, blank faces, or a few bland responses. For one thing, your team members may not be aware they are falling short of their collaborative potential and thus see no need to address the problem. Even if they do, they still may be unwilling to address it, because they fear retribution, feel embarrassed, or simply want to avoid looking stupid.

Researchers Amy Edmondson and Jim Detert have shown that people are hard-wired to evade perceived threats to their psychological or material well-being.[6] Inspiring others to devote their best effort to a task is hard enough, but just encouraging them to share their true thoughts and feelings about it might be even harder. As much as you would like your colleagues to leave their egos at the door and focus solely on doing the right thing for the team and the organization, the ego is a constant companion who never takes time off or waits patiently outside the conference room.

In order to be successful in the second step of the process, you have to create a psychologically safe space for your team to have tough conversations and push each other to become a high performing team.

Even when teams start by establishing commitments, like the Diamondbacks did, they often experience a growing gap between what their team *says* and what it *does*. We call it the *saying-doing gap*, and it is the reason why most teams never push the metaphorical boulder as hard as they could. Changing behaviors to close the saying-doing gap is the third step in the process (Figure I.3).

Figure I.3   The 3 Teamwork Steps

To recap the 3x3 framework: (1) You first need to get your team to **Commit** to goals, roles, and norms. (2) You need to regularly **Check** alignment with these commitments. 3) Finally, you need to **Close** the gap between saying and doing.

"How Have You Helped a Pharm Rep Today?"

Time and again, we have observed many examples of leaders who have successfully implemented the 3x3 Framework to close the saying-doing gap and supercharge performance. Take Jenny, the vice president of strategy for a major pharmaceutical company, who was tasked with being the architect of a transformational change initiative that we studied. At the time we interviewed Jenny, she had been an integral part of transforming the company's culture by reorienting its entire business model to focus on customer satisfaction rather than sales volume.

Responding to the passage of the Affordable Care Act as well as increasingly stringent restrictions on pharmaceutical sales, the leaders of the company—let's call it PharmTec—concluded they had to adapt to a changing healthcare landscape. Jenny was charged with leading the team that would develop a multi-step initiative to center business decisions and performance on the needs and concerns of healthcare professionals. Above all, PharmTec leaders wanted to change the culture of the company, one shared by many others in the industry, which rewarded sales reps for promoting prescriptions above all else.

Jenny's team created a five-year road map and an 11-point plan. They developed new goals, roles, and norms for the company's sales team. The plan was airtight, and employees seemed to respond to the new values espoused by the president in company-wide meetings. But Jenny noticed that something was off when she walked the PharmTec hallways to see whether employees were actually aligned with the initiative. She noticed that while the sales team managers parroted the values of the new practitioner-focused mindset, some still had plaques on their desks saying, "How have you helped a pharm rep today?" They were still regaling new hires with stories about reps who had the best sales figures and seemed to favor them in promotions and reviews. In other words, there was a gap between what they said when they recited the new values and what they did in continuing to incentivize sales volume.

Once she spotted this gap, Jenny's team went about closing it. Managers attended workshops that instilled the rules involved with evaluating rep behaviors under the new system. This training focused on the most basic elements of the new behaviors, such as how to properly observe sales teams in the field. PharmTec leaders invited physicians who were enthusiastic about the new business model to speak at company meetings. Insiders and outsiders began telling stories highlighting the behaviors of reps who had gone out of their way to help a practitioner. These stories tapped into a powerful motivator of change—pride. They also served as reminders that the reps who did the best job of serving their customers would be rewarded and that the reps who merely generated volume were following the old rules.

Jenny's team led a successful rollout of the new initiative. Internal surveys showed a jump in employee morale, and physicians who had seen PharmTec as just another big pharma company began valuing the different approach their reps took. To achieve this change, Jenny followed the three steps we have outlined. First, her team members established commitments around new goals, roles, and processes. Then they identified the conflicting rules that caused misalignments between those commitments and actual sales team behaviors. Finally, they cultivated new habits and ideals to close the saying-doing gap.

Jenny's team felt its way through this process, basically using trial-and-error techniques. In this book, we teach you to do it systematically so that adjusting team culture becomes second nature. Getting your team to create new behaviors is hard, but with practice you can get better at it.

How This Book Is Organized

In the following chapters, we give you the tools and techniques to establish commitments on your team, check on the alignment of behaviors with the commitments, and close the saying-doing gap. The process will help your team stay deeply engaged and perform to the maximum of its potential.

Before we describe how this book is organized, however, let us pause to reflect on a skeptical thought that might be bothering you at this moment. You might be wondering whether the best strategy for getting something done, and done right, is to just do it yourself, especially since experts have gathered loads of data that raise questions about the effectiveness of teams. True, individuals are often more effective than teams in performing certain tasks that require high degrees of creativity or technical knowledge. But it would be a terrible mistake to give up on teams, because they actually accomplish amazing things every day in organizations around the world. And your team can, too. So, to return to the question we started the chapter with: "Can I make my team work?," we answer with confidence: "You can!" Based on our research and experience, we have concluded that the path to becoming a true HPT is our field-tested process for relentlessly closing the saying-doing gap.

Part One of this book describes the 3x3 framework (see Figure I.4).

- *Chapter 1* provides a detailed explanation of the first step in the process: establishing commitments. We describe a highly structured way of having discussions with your team members in this phase, which we call *chartering*. HPTs create a charter that guides their work.

- *Chapter 2* shows how you can create the conditions for checking the alignment between saying and doing—the second step of the

Figure I.4   The 3x3 Framework

process. The goal is to identify your team's hidden problems and stay on top of the natural drift that all teams experience. Outside observers often have unique insights into others' cultures, and HPTs know how to become their own observers and identify the behaviors that help close the saying-doing gap.

- *Chapter 3* describes a detailed behavioral process designed to close the saying-doing gap: STAR. It stands for be Specific, Take small steps, Alter your environment, and be a Realistic optimist.

- *Chapter 4* reviews the seven deadly sins of teamwork: the most common bad habits that teams develop, often without being aware of them. We walk team leaders through ways to break down each of these barriers to performance.

Part Two of this book analyzes five common team types: their defining characteristics, their biggest problems, and key behaviors that produce success. Why are we focusing on these five? Based on our experience as consultants and business school faculty, we bet you spend a good chunk of your time collaborating in ways that resemble one or more of them.

- *Chapter 5* provides best practices for leading virtual teams. Virtual teams always need to work especially hard to create cohesion and maintain engagement, but there are ways to make it easier.

- *Chapter 6* shows how startups and entrepreneurial teams can successfully manage the team-formation process even when they have to move at breakneck speed.

- *Chapter 7* aims to correct common misperceptions about project teams that need to be creative and innovative in addition to being productive.

- *Chapter 8* analyzes the dynamics of top teams. These teams are often made up of all high-performing leaders who need to learn when to follow and how to leverage the power of social networks to augment their formal authority.

- *Chapter 9* seeks to refresh some typical ways of thinking about committees. Rather than laboring to direct a group of people who are collaborating because they *have to*, you can create a team that *wants to be* high performing.

- Our *Conclusion* explains why today's workplace demands that all teams be high performing and that everybody know how to be a high-performing teammate.

HPT Takeaways

Focus on the Three Foundations

For many reasons and in many ways, groups undershoot their potential. To become HPTs, they must first establish the Three Foundations: Goals, Roles, and Norms. The Foundations are based on commitments made by team members to each other.

Make the rules

Human beings make rules to problem-solve and to organize themselves around tasks. The rules become ingrained and form the basis of culture. Rule-making is the first step in the 3x3 Framework (Commit/Check/Close) that leads to high performance.

Watch for the Saying-Doing Gap

Productive team cultures are aligned with the tasks that need to be done and with the environment in which a team does its work. Lack of alignment leads to the saying-doing gap. All teams have to manage this problem. HPTs do it by periodically checking their behavioral alignment with stated commitments and the environment. HPTs address misalignments by taking small steps to close the gap between saying and doing.

COMMITTED TEAMS

Part One

The first part of this book is about the basics: creating a collaborative culture that ignites passion and supercharges team performance. Chapters 1 through 3 describe the three-steps of the 3×3 Framework—Commit, Check, and Close. You can apply this process to any kind of team. Each chapter includes examples and tools that make it easy for you to apply key takeaways. The final chapter identifies seven of the most common mistakes that undermine teamwork and offers strategies for correcting them.

1 Commit: To Know the Rules, You Have to Make Them

Even a lone genius needs help from a team.

British mathematician Alan Turing[1] learned this lesson in his race to crack the sophisticated code used by the German military in World War II. Turing was the consummate rogue intellectual, a brilliant savant who foresaw the modern computer and the advent of artificial intelligence. He envisioned a machine that could use algorithms to solve any mathematical problem. But when the British government tapped him to join an elite team of cryptographers tasked with deciphering the famous German Enigma machine, he balked.

Turing was famous for being socially awkward and eccentric. He was known to hold his pants up with string and ride his bicycle to work with a gas mask during allergy season. He at first believed that working in a group would only slow him down. But he eventually came to appreciate the collective capabilities of his fellow mathematicians in the secretive "Hut 8" of the government's central code-breaking station. The group succeeded in besting the most powerful cipher machine in the world because the right foundations for team success were laid, ensuring the output of the whole would be more than the sum of its parts.

In other words, Turing and his group of cryptographers established the rules that created a culture of high-performing teamwork.

For starters, the team was committed to a clear common goal of cracking the German code in a highly distinctive way. Rather than seeking to uncover an underlying structure, it involved identifying probable words in Axis messages and working backward to decipher discrete meanings. This gave the team a central focus around which all of its activities and discussions could be organized.

The team also defined roles that tapped into the personalities, skills, and interests of each individual. The mathematician Alexander Hugh came onto the team as Turing's deputy. But Turing eventually let Hugh take over the team when it became clear that Turing's talents were wasted by having to manage the administrative aspects of Hut 8. By stepping into the leadership post, Hugh enabled Turing to focus his energy where he could provide the most value to the team.

Turing also benefited from working with Stewart Menzies, the head of Britain's intelligence agency and a crucial liaison for the Hut 8 team to the rest of the military administration. In stark contrast to Turing, Menzies was a classic *bon vivant*. The grandson of a wealthy whiskey distiller, he was known for his easy-going personality as well as his multiple marriages. Winston Churchill was skeptical of Menzies' abilities when he was appointed head of MI6, but Menzies eventually won Churchill over and became a part of his inner circle. Menzies' knack for building relationships with key people was crucial to gaining support and resources for Hut 8's activities.

The team was full of oddballs who were more accustomed to getting things done on their own. One of the cryptographers was known for taking long walks to think by himself and then throwing his coffee mug in the nearby lake when he was finished. Strange conduct notwithstanding, between 1939 and 1941, the team solved the puzzle created by the most complicated encoding machine the world had ever seen and shortened the length of the war by years. To do it, Turing had to create a culture that enabled his team to thrive. Essential to its success was the special rules that connected a larger purpose to particular behaviors and habits.

For example, one of those behavioral rules had to do with identifying bottlenecks and immediately alerting decision-makers about them, even if the team had to work outside of the established bureaucratic structure. In an exchange dramatized in the popular Hollywood film about Turing, "The Imitation Game,"[2] every member of the team signed a note sent directly to Churchill about four specific resource needs, one of them being the shortage of trained typists. It was highly unusual to forward this sort of request directly to the British Prime Minister, to say the least. But Churchill swiftly granted all of the team's requests and the work proceeded apace.

Making Commitments: The Power of Structured Conversation

What made Turing and his band of loner intellectuals a successful team? Recall the story of how Jenny from PharmTec got her sales teams on track. Though Jenny and Turing were operating in obviously different environments, what they have in common is a need to be explicit about the rules governing team behavior. It is just too easy to become committed to the wrong ones. Jenny became aware of this problem only after her change initiative sputtered out of the gate, hampered by the old habits that remained unchanged at her company. You can avoid this headache by developing the right rules collaboratively as soon as your team forms.

Of course, the basic question is: What rules should you establish? The first step in the process is all about committing to the rules that *matter*. Research on teams tells us that these fall into three categories, or what we have called the Three Foundations: Goals, Roles, and Norms (see Figure 1.1). HPTs establish those foundations by having

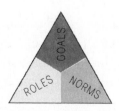

Figure 1.1   The Three Foundations

a structured conversation. Our research has shown that conversation is simply the best tool for organizing collaboration and making commitments.

The outcome of your conversation is what management scholar Leigh Thompson[3] calls a team charter. A team charter can be something formal you write on a piece of paper and post, or it can be as simple as a set of verbal agreements. The key is having a conversation about concrete commitments you can refer to later and hold one another accountable for. In the Resources section, we have provided you with a checklist of questions you should be considering to create effective goals, roles and norms. You can begin with talking about any of the foundations, but you should make sure to address all three. The more explicit you are in identifying specifics, milestones, and metrics, the easier it will be to translate commitments into actions and make adjustments later on. But the reality is that it will take some time—and several conversations—to dig down to a level of detail that reveals the behaviors needed for success.

Let's look at how you can structure a chartering process for your own team.

Goals: Grounding Vision in Practice

One of the most important steps you can take in forming a team is to establish the rules about the team's vision and direction: what goals you will pursue as well as what is outside of your scope.

This is hard enough under the best of circumstances. But imagine how hard it is to do goal-setting with someone who would rather not even be part of the team. That was the situation faced by one of our simulation teams at Wharton, Yellow Lightning, in its very first meeting. We were facilitating an ice-breaker, asking each of the participants why they had come to Wharton and what they wanted to get out of their two weeks together. The conversation flowed smoothly as each member spoke to the importance of learning new skills and developing relationships—until it was Ankur's turn to talk.

Ankur, an energetic and intense principal at a top consulting firm, had only known his fellow EDP participants for a day, but he had already developed a reputation for bluntness. When asked about his own personal goals, he stayed true to form, telling his teammates that he had been forced to participate in EDP and that he had little to learn from the simulation. He felt pressured to wrap up a time-sensitive issue that his colleagues back at the office were waiting on, and he made the calculation that it was better for him to placate his real team than worry about supporting the simulated one he would be stuck with for two weeks. His flippant attitude set the tone for the first part of the exercise. Ankur would alternate being arrogantly overbearing and being completely disengaged. He often became engrossed with his iPhone while others deliberated.

WIIFM?   What can we learn from Ankur's example? Start with the widely accepted claim: to be successful, every team needs strong, collective goals that members can rally around. Research has repeatedly identified this as one of the fundamental conditions of team success. Intuitively, this makes sense, since individual team members need to align their efforts and shared goals help facilitate alignment. In his book *Collaboration*, U.C. Berkeley management professor Morten Hansen[4] calls a central goal the "unifying lever" of teams, and he urges leaders to make use of it. Sound enough advice, but one of the lessons from Ankur's relationship to his team is that, paradoxically, in order for team members to put the collective goals first, they have to feel there is a clear answer to the WIIFM question: What's in it for me?

Yellow Lightning had lofty goals of learning and self-improvement, but this was not enough to engage Ankur because he felt this vision for the team was of little use to him. Ankur's attitude may be extreme, but it is not uncommon. How many times have you been on a team with someone who was compelled to be there by the higher-ups and thought it was a waste of his or her time? Even when all the members of a team genuinely want to participate, their motivations are often highly diverse. They may have a personal stake in the outcome of the team's efforts because it affects their own unit; or they may be seeking visibility in the organization; or they want to learn a specific set of skills. If these individual aspirations are not met through the team's work, they could easily become free-riders and ultimately cause the group to underperform, no matter how lofty its vision may be.

Our experience shows that team members are much more likely to embrace collective goals when they are aligned with personal goals and motivations. Like Ankur, we all navigate interconnected "webs of significance"—Clifford Geertz's phrase[5] for our multiple commitments—because you belong to different groups with their own values, goals, and demands: the office, your home, the workshop team. You don't just let go of one group's set of concerns when you move to another group. The ties of these webs persist wherever you go and create areas of harmony or conflict with one another.

For just this reason, the goal-setting processes that are a critical aspect of team formation have to begin with a conversation—even a negotiation—about individual goals. When our teams first meet, we like them to start with a simple question: Why are you here?

It may sound straightforward, but the answers we hear tell us a lot about what is motivating each individual as well as what their expectations are for the experience. The answers tend to fall into two categories: they are usually either developmental—for example, an executive in accounting might be aiming to improve her leadership capabilities—or they are about creating a certain impact in the organization, the market, or society.

Developmental Goals
Learn about the different functions in my business unit
Sharpen my leadership skills
Get a better understanding of modeling software

Impact Goals
Improve the bottom line of my business unit
Increase morale in my team
Create demand in the market for this innovative product

The process of checking and aligning individual goals with team goals thus does as much to support team performance as it benefits individuals. Of course, it is not always possible to close this gap completely, but even the act of trying will often foster engagement, honesty, and trust among team members. This is how Yellow Lightning eventually got through to Ankur and made him into a contributor. When he initially announced his lack of interest in the team, others were unsure of how to handle it. Yet as the rounds went on, they saw that he would light up and turn away from his phone for certain types of decision-making discussions, particularly those oriented around strategy, which was his personal forte and area of expertise within his firm.

Noticing this, the team began increasingly tapping Ankur to take the lead on developing customer retention and revenue growth strategies. He began turning to his iPhone less and less while becoming increasingly engaged and enthusiastic about his role on the team, offering support in an area where he had more expertise than any other member. Through this process of goal alignment, Ankur went from being deadweight to a productive force.

If/Then Thinking   Even the most well-aligned goals will encounter barriers. While you will never anticipate every setback, you can put your team on solid footing by engaging in if/then thinking during the chartering process. If/then thinking deals with a potential problem by identifying what you will do *if* you encounter it. This is one of the defining characteristics of people who are able to consistently attain their goals, as University of Utrecht researchers discovered[6] when they studied different strategies for changing eating habits. The researchers found that people who anticipated temptations (by proactively creating so-called *replacement* strategies) were more successful than those who simply tried to ignore temptations.

In a similar way, David Allen, creator of the popular Getting Things Done[7] productivity system, has structured his whole approach around the recognition that you inevitably struggle to focus on the right

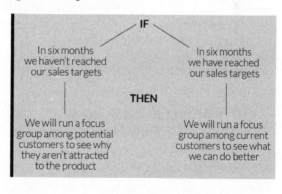

task at the right time that will maximize your efficiency. His heralded task-management system pushes you to anticipate barriers and create a plan in advance so that your efforts are targeted where they can be most effective.

What these insights tap into is the common notion that you are more likely to deal with challenges if you plan for them in advance rather than waiting to grapple with them in the heat of the moment. As you set goals with your team, we encourage you to do more than write a set of milestones down on paper. Imagine the likely issues that could derail your success and create rules for managing them.

Roles: How Do the Pieces Fit Together?

In addition to goals, teams need rules determining what each person does within the team. In other words, teams need roles. Research on team performance and workplace productivity consistently finds that teams work harder and better when members have clear, interdependent roles that tap into their skills, expertise, and sense of meaning. J. Richard Hackman identifies this as one of the main differentiators between a real team and a collection of people working in parallel, or what he calls a "co-acting group."[8]

HPTs establish clear and differentiated roles. To start, you should make sure you have the basics: the skill sets and kinds of expertise needed to achieve desired outcomes. In our simulations, the teams that do best have finance, negotiation, and marketing skill sets represented among the team members. The particular skill–expertise mix may be different on your team, but the point is that you should have a mix and know what it is.

Team members should also consider how they want to shape their roles based on how they derive meaning from work. Researchers Amy Wrzesniewski and Jane E. Dutton call this "job-crafting."[9] It helps people develop a positive self-image, have a sense of autonomy, and connect with others in the workplace—three fundamental ways in which people become passionate in their work. Involving team members in shaping their roles will not only boost their enthusiasm, it will also enhance the quality of their work.

In addition to finding the right fit between individual team members and their roles, you should also consider how all of the roles fit together to form a team's structure. Every team develops in its own unique way, but in general we find team cultures are differentiated along two major spectrums:

1. Are they more *hierarchical* or *flat*? This axis is all about the distribution of authority within the team. Hierarchical teams give more authority to a strong leader, whereas authority is more widely distributed among the members in a flatter team.

2. Are they more *individualistic* or *more cohesive*? This axis characterizes the team's working relationships. Individualistic teams tend to have more transactional exchanges, while cohesive ones interact in more personal ways.

To discover your own team cultural archetype (see Figure 1.2), take the Team Culture Assessment in the Resources section. The survey will help you determine which of the following categories you should use to describe your team.

Troops (low on cohesion, high on hierarchy)   The team Steve Jobs assembled to produce the iPhone falls into this quadrant. He assembled the company's superstars, pitting them against each other under the threat of being blamed for product failures. The team was heavily individualistic, but committed to Jobs's vision, which eventually

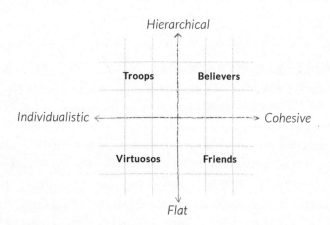

Figure 1.2   Team Cultural Archetypes

produced a breakthrough product. The strength of this team type is in the common direction provided by a strong leader. The downside is the lack of feedback, since team members work in siloes and aim mainly to serve the leader.

Believers (high on cohesion, high on hierarchy)   Facebook is characterized by an iconic leader in Mark Zuckerberg (and increasingly Sheryl Sandberg as well) but also a cohesive bond between employees around a strong culture of experimentation embodied in the phrase "the hacker way." Believer cultures like the predominant one at Facebook are energized and rally around a compelling vision, but they can easily succumb to groupthink.

Virtuosos (low on cohesion, low on hierarchy)   In 2003, Phil Jackson added basketball legends Gary Payton and Karl Malone to a Lakers team that already featured Kobe Bryant and Shaquille O'Neal, two future Hall-of-Famers. The team of big egos stormed through the regular season and play-offs but sputtered out in the NBA finals that year, winning only one game against the Detroit Pistons, a team with much less star power at that point but a great deal of team chemistry. Like that Lakers team, Virtuosos benefit from having the talent to take on big challenges with gusto, but the lack of team rapport or a strong leader can cause them to pull apart under duress.

Friends (high on cohesion, low on hierarchy)   W.L. Gore is one of the few large companies with relatively little top-down structure. The 10,000 employees make decisions on everything from projects to hiring through self-managing teams of 8 to 12 people. As CEO Terri Kelly says:[10] "It's far better to rely upon a broad base of individuals and leaders who share a common set of values and feel personal ownership for the overall success of the organization. These responsible and empowered individuals will serve as much better watchdogs than any single, dominant leader or bureaucratic structure." Research on leadership styles shows that this empowering approach can pay dividends in the long run, since team members become highly engaged and collaborative. In the short run, though, these teams get a slower start as individuals take time to achieve a high comfort level with each other and their roles.

There is no one right structure. The important thing is to be aware of the trade-offs with each one and to shape the structure that best fits your team and its goals. In the early stages of team formation, your discussions will be fairly abstract, but they will get deeper as your team gains more experience working together. In the next chapter, we give you the tools to assess and consider the benefits and challenges of the structure that your team develops over time.

As examples of different ways to organize, compare the structure of two HPTs we worked with in our EDP laboratory:

1. Team Red Alert was led by a strong figure, Paul, who as a former Navy SEAL could be called "combative" in more ways than one. Paul led his team like a platoon, barking commands at his reports to get them on task. He even had a physically dominating presence when he was in the room, standing and pacing around as others sat down, pecking away at computers or poring over spreadsheets. In frequently reaffirming his commitment to "being bold," he tapped into his experience as a member of an elite fighting unit. He made the vast majority of the decisions for the team, and during group discussions his primary goal was to articulate a vision and get others on board.

2. Contrast Paul to the leader of the Orange Glow, the soft-spoken Jim, who was much more of a facilitator than the strong-willed Navy SEAL. Jim made consensus a priority, and would take the time to ask each person how he or she felt about a decision before he gave it the green light, even when time was tight. It was important to Jim that everyone feel ownership of even seemingly minor decisions. He believed that development of the team dynamic over the long term was more important than winning on a round-by-round basis. While Paul made his voice heard continuously, Jim would go silent and sometimes physically step back from team members while they were finalizing a task, taking

care not to disturb their thought process. Although English was not the native language of most of the team members, Orange Glow saw linguistic diversity as an asset and not a liability. To this team, it meant that each person would have to work to clearly articulate his or her thinking and that they would have to listen to each other even more carefully.

Whereas Paul crafted a team with a fairly hierarchical structure, Jim led a relatively flat group. They could not have been more different, but both teams were high-performing from start to finish, landing among the top three groups in every round. The key was understanding how skill sets, areas of expertise, and personalities interacted, and then creating a role structure that optimized the interactions of these factors. One team valued the clarity of purpose provided by Paul; the other valued the space for equitable contribution and thoughtful dialogue created by Jim. It is also important to recognize that there are trade-offs in any structure. Red Alert's team members felt that at times the lack of dissent in the room led to less well-informed decisions. The Orange Glow team, on the other hand, had difficulty making quick decisions, and at times their external business partners felt out of the loop and devalued.

In considering your own team type and structure, you should assess whether a strong vision and delegation from the top or a more informal structure will contribute to peak performance. You should also consider whether you are better off working in interconnected silos, or tackling each task collaboratively. Having this conversation early on, using our two-axis framework, will help you start defining and organizing roles in a way that promotes team success down the road.

Norms: Making the Behavioral Rules That Matter

Your team structure is related to the third foundation: norms. If goals are about where your team is going and roles describe what you will do to get there, norms are the rules governing how you interact to fulfill both goals and roles. Our experience tells us that these rules tend to fall into three major buckets, each of which prompts a question: How do we resolve conflicts? How do we communicate? How do we decide? Managing differences, sharing information, and acting on it are the three fundamental processes in which teams engage.

Conflict   Having good norms of communication is different from just getting along as a team. While there is nothing wrong with team members being friendly to each other, a surface-level politeness can cover over a deeper lack of trust that interferes with constructive dialogue. Not only do HPTs learn to accept conflict, they understand that productive tension can sometimes be the most important driver of creative thinking and unorthodox solutions.

Management scholars Bill Fischer and Andy Boynton have conducted extensive research[11] on what they call "virtuoso teams" (a term we borrow for our cultural archetype above)—distinctive groups, like the team behind the Manhattan Project and the creators of *West Side Story*, that came together under high-pressure circumstances and produced revolutionary results in their field. Fischer and Boynton have found that, on these teams of high performers, the egos tend to be big and the dialogue intense. But even the most combative group can create amazing collaborative results if the competitive dynamic is undergirded by a commitment to a common vision as well as mutual trust and respect.

Such was the nature of the famously discordant duo of John Lennon and Paul McCartney. John and Paul could hardly have been more different in their personalities and public image. John was the disorganized, disheveled rebel, famously prickly with the press and willing to sacrifice the accessibility of his music for genre-breaking experimentation. Paul played the role of clean-cut diplomat, with a knack for crafting digestible, crowd-pleasing tunes and a concern with grooming the band's public image.

The standard narrative about the pair's musical trajectory is that, as their conflict intensified, they became increasingly independent songwriters, creating brilliant music on their own in spite of each other. But writer Joshua Shenk argues[12] that even as the band seemed to be falling apart and the relationship between the two became tense, their songs were a collaborative product, a result of their ability to push each other to achieve new creative heights. For example, Paul recounted in an interview the way John challenged him as he wrote the song "Getting Better": "I was sitting there doing 'Getting better all the time,' and John just said, in his laconic way, 'It couldn't get no worse.' And I thought, Oh, brilliant! This is exactly why I love writing with John."

The pair's stylistic clashes made them each better songwriters than they would have been on their own and the creative tension propelled the band to become one of the most popular and influential musical teams of all time.

The key to channeling this intense energy into collaborative results rather than destructive competition was the respect they had cultivated for each other and a mutual trust that both were striving toward a common goal of producing great music. Even today, Paul still uses his memory of John as a creative muse, as he described in a *Rolling Stone* interview:[13] "If I'm at a point where I go, 'I'm not sure about this,' I'll throw it across the room to John. He'll say, 'You can't go there, man.' And I'll say, 'You're quite right. How about this?' 'Yeah, that's better.' We'll have a conversation. I don't want to lose that."

Good goal-setting will take you a long way toward developing a sense of shared accountability and mutual investment in the team, but another key ingredient of strong rapport is an understanding of your team's attitudes toward conflict. During the commitments chartering process, you should have a conversation with your teammates about how each of you handles contentious issues. We recommend discussing examples of teams that encountered conflict and sharing feelings about how it was resolved. To start your discussion, you might even consider sharing the stories about the Lennon-McCartney partnership and virtuoso teams that we have told. Reflecting on your team members' reactions will help anticipate style conflicts and prepare you for how to respond productively when they arise. If/then thinking, which you employed in shaping goals, can be useful in creating conflict-management strategies, as well.

Communication   Our perspective on communication comes from the work done by one of us with our Wharton colleague, Richard Shell.[14] You can dig a lot deeper into that research in the book, *The Art of Woo: Using Strategic Persuasion to Sell Your Ideas,* but here we want to highlight one of the key Woo concepts: people have distinctive preferences for how they like to give and receive information. In other words, they communicate on different "channels".

You should be aware of the channel you are using in sharing information. Imagine, for example, you were making a case to your teammates about investing in a new technology. You have several options:

Authority   Deliberately call attention to your professional status to make your point with extra force. Teammates might respond positively to this kind of authoritative style—or not, depending on how they relate to authority.

Data   Refer to research studies and market analyses. Data-oriented teammates would find you persuasive if you communicated this way.

Relationships   Make an emotional connection. Teammates who value relationships want to feel an emotional connection with you. For those tuned into the relationships channel, data is less persuasive than rapport.

Interests   Lead with a point about WIIFM. Some people are always asking WIIFM and respond best to proposals that serve their interests.

Vision   Appeal to higher goals. At least some of your teammates are likely to feel motivated and engaged when you appeal to values like those expressed in a vision statement or even in the original team charter.

Politics   Show political savvy. The "politicians" on you team pay most attention to you when you are talking about how to engage key people and groups across your organization.

In summary, there are multiple channels of communication. *The Art of Woo* describes the preceding six. More generally, if you want to get your point across to a teammate, tune in to the right channel. You may have to experiment until you find it.

Even a team with language barriers like the Orange Glow can become strong communicators if people understand each other's styles and adapt accordingly. The Orange Glow had more introverts than extroverts, and the introverts had to be cajoled to speak up. The team created norms related to giving each person space to contribute ideas and listening carefully to their contributions. The team without a common language ended up being among the best communicators we have seen in our simulation research.

When you share preferences for giving and getting information, you reduce the likelihood that discussions will founder on misunderstandings. This also helps instill good communication habits that boost your team's performance.

Making Decisions   In addition to discussing conflict and communication, you will also need to consider a critical question that bears on action. Namely, how are you going to decide? Plenty of teams struggle with this issue, especially when they are made up of peers. But you should have a conversation about it. If you fail to set the rules for decision-making, they will form organically and often produce unintended consequences.

Bad decision-making can affect the "smartest" of teams. Behavioral experts Cass Sunstein and Reid Hastie[15] note that even teams with a disproportionately high IQ can make bad decisions because they neglect to pay attention to how they manage discussions. This can lead to the wrong information getting amplified in a group when, for example, the first person to speak controls the conversation whether he or she is right or wrong, or someone succumbs to groupthink without checking his or her biases. Sunstein and Reid recommend mitigating these tendencies by finding ways to create an environment in which unique and contradictory information is valued over me-too opinions. As with nearly every aspect of team culture, there is no one right way to manage the group. The most important thing is to be aware of *how* you manage it.

Considering a few basic questions will help your team be clear about how it handles decision-making:

1. Do we have enough diversity of thought?

    If teammates come from similar professional or educational backgrounds, then diversity may be lacking. Soliciting input from specialists and other informed outsiders can introduce divergent views into the decision-making process.

2. Are we comfortable expressing differences of opinion?

    Attitudes toward conflict obviously affect how groups discuss differences. If your team on the whole seems conflict-averse, you should consider assigning one person the "devil's advocate" role when tough decisions are being vetted. This will increase the chances that both "pros" and "cons" will be expressed.

3. Do we have a way to reach closure?

    When the time is right to drive toward a conclusion, teams have several options for getting there. One is to take a vote, Another is to assign one person the "right" to make a decision on a particular issue. A third is to rely on consensus—basically, continuing to discuss an issue until everyone is in agreement, just as Philadelphia's Quakers have done for centuries

A Few Essential Norms   While you might be tempted to come up with a laundry list of norms, it is best to focus on a few rules that will have the greatest impact. These are ones related to resolving conflicts, communicating, and making decisions.

The television producer Glen Mazzara[16] found this to be the case when he asked the women on his own writing team why they didn't speak up more. Mazzara is most recently known for his work on the popular series *The Walking Dead,* but he got his first big break as a producer with the show *The Shield*. He had worked his way up as a writer, first breaking through on the team of the Don Johnson series *Nash Bridges* before coming to *The Shield* as a senior editor in 2002. After the show took off, Mazzara was promoted in its second season, eventually rising to become the executive producer.

As a leader, Mazzara emphasized inclusiveness in meetings with his team of writers. In an interview, he bluntly articulated his philosophy of constructive dialogue: "Do not knock something off the table unless you are going to replace it. Do not just piss on someone's idea without offering one better. That's not fair. That's not kind. That's not respectful and that's not your job. Your job is to generate ideas."

Mazzara's goal of fostering an environment of inclusive decision-making hit a snag when he realized that two of his younger female writers would stay quiet during meetings while the men dominated the floor. Pulling them aside, he asked why they weren't speaking up. "Watch what happens when we do," they told him. Mazzara paid careful attention to the team dynamic the next time they got together for a brainstorming session and what he saw made him understand the young women's apprehension. Whenever they threw out an idea, one of the men on the team would interrupt them, shooting them down or building on the idea without their input.

At that moment, Mazzara observed an all-too-common phenomenon discussed by Sheryl Sandberg[17] in her book *Lean In*. Many teams, like the writers of *The Shield,* operate by an unwritten and often unconscious rule that men should be the decision-makers. We see this play out in work settings where women who try to take the lead are viewed negatively. In this case, rather than rock the boat, the female writers had opted to sit back and let the men decide the direction of the show.

Seeing this, Mazzara cleverly laid down a norm for the whole team without calling out the gender dynamic. He instituted a rule that no one would interrupt another person while they were pitching an idea for the show. By focusing on one rule that really mattered for the team's success and making it explicit, Mazzara spurred more equitable contributions from the women on his team and the quality of the show benefited as a result.

How can you write effective rules for your team? Focus on the top three to five things that you think will be most important for the team dynamic based on what you know about your particular group. To determine what these might be, go back to the potential barriers you identified in your engagement-building process. Creating norms that head off those challenges are likely to be your most important priorities. If women on your team raised the possibility of gender disparities in discussion air-times based on their past experience, you might create a no-interruptions rule similar to Mazzara's. Understanding individual styles and then creating the few rules that really matter for channeling those styles into productive dialogue will place your group in a strong position to weather the inevitable storms of conflict, dissent, and discontent that any team faces.

Don't Stop!

Many teams forget about the foundations once they have been defined, but we encourage you to see the discussion about commitments as an ongoing process, not a one-time event. Misalignments in the rules you have made are bound to occur, because the nature of team culture is to be in constant flux.

HPT Takeaways

Charter first

Team chartering is a method for discussing the Three Foundations. A charter discussion is highly structured, focusing on goals, roles, and norms.

Anticipate barriers to goals

Goal-setting is most effective when it is combined with If/Then thinking to anticipate barriers.

Create interdependent roles

Teams are different from "co-acting groups," where people work in parallel rather than interacting in defined ways. HPTs carefully define roles and periodically check whether the team buys into the definitions.

Norms

The most important teamwork norms provide guidelines for sharing information, making decisions, and resolving conflicts.

In the next chapter, we turn to the second step of the 3x3. This is when you work on cultivating the right mindset for identifying these misalignments before they sap your team's performance.

2 Check: What You Don't Know Is Probably Hurting You

"What does Shakespeare have to teach the business world?"

The professor pondered the question. Hedging, he noted that he was not a businessperson himself, but after thinking a moment he added: "I find that reading Shakespeare is like *overhearing* yourself." He paused to think again, and then he elaborated to the interviewer from the *Harvard Business Review*: "Your reader might reflect how often she herself is conscious of the will to change after she has the surprise of overhearing herself."

The professor was the literary critic and MacArthur Prize winner Harold Bloom,[1] who teaches at Yale. HBR wanted to know why Bill Gates and other business luminaries should be reading the great works of literature. How would it help them run their companies and manage teams? Bloom's answer underscored the importance of reflection in adjusting habits of thought and action.

For HPTs, reflection is the core activity in the second step of the 3x3: checking on alignment. Teams often underperform because people fall out of sync with one another and their environment.

The result: lack of follow-through on commitments, or the goals, roles, and norms that drive team performance. HPTs are conscious of the stresses and strains that lead to misalignment, course-correcting in response to changing circumstances.

Making commitments and course-correcting. Simple? Far from it. Course-correcting is much easier said than done: the course that you are on is often hard to see. As we noted in the introduction, the difficulty lies in the basic human tendency to create problem-solving rules without being completely aware of them. So let's look closely at what social science tells us about this surprising phenomenon and examine why it matters to your team.

Team Culture and the Mystery of the Kaiko

Another pig sacrifice? Anthropologist Roy Rappaport had seen enough of this ritual.[2] He felt it was a distraction from his dissertation research. He was only interested in studying agriculture and nutrition among the Maring tribe of Papua, New Guinea.

To gather data, Rappaport relied upon a simple tool: a scale to weigh the food that the Maring brought home from hunting and foraging. As the villagers were sitting down to a meal, he would ask them to pause so that he could enter information into his notebooks. From time to time, the Maring would slaughter a pig to honor their ancestors, before they started eating. Called the *kaiko,* the ritual began to annoy Rappaport, because he had to sit and wait until it was over before he could get on with his pressing work. During his first few months in New Guinea, concentrating on keeping detailed records of caloric intake and dietary preferences, he failed to understand how the ceremony actually helped address a significant problem.

Anthropologists have built an entire discipline around observing the rules that groups use to solve problems. These rules—often expressed through the collective symbols and behaviors that define a culture—are so taken for granted that even an outside observer may not see them at first. A case in point was Rappaport's experience among the Maring. When he first began doing his dissertation research, he failed to see that one of the most fundamental drivers of Maring social life was right under his nose. It took him months to make sense of what he was seeing.

Rappaport arrived in 1960 at the village he would end up studying for decades. The young PhD student experienced instant culture shock when he started living there, far from his own tribe of academics at Columbia University. He quickly realized how difficult it would be to interpret behaviors among a completely new and unfamiliar group of people. He described his early time in the field as "a total buzzing confusion."

After a few months, Rappaport noticed that the *kaiko* tended to happen around outbreaks of war. He also observed that this coincided with growth in the pig population. Mapping the growth onto his nutritional and harvest data, he realized that in times of harmony among the Maring villages, the population increased to an unsustainable size. A hungry pig ate almost as much as an adult human. As the number of pigs grew, they took up land and devoured crops. Before long, they strained the region's resources and created tension between neighboring villages. When war eventually broke out, the *kaikos* would bring the pig population back down to manageable levels and social harmony would be reestablished.

Rappaport surmised that the *kaiko* was about much more than offerings to the ancestors. It was also a means of intelligently managing the region's resources and maintaining social stability among the villages. But this relationship between resource management and ritual was so ingrained in everyday life that the Maring failed to mention it when Rappaport asked them about the *kaiko*. They talked about ancestors, not population control. The perspective was so pervasive and taken for granted that Rappaport himself ignored for several months what would eventually be the central focus of his findings.

When he later explained his thinking to the Maring, they greeted his interpretation with their version of "Imagine that!" His explanation made sense to them, but they had never thought of it themselves and had never put it in words. The *kaiko* was just an expression of the way they did things.

The beauty of culture is that it enables all of us to accomplish extraordinary feats through collaboration without even knowing how we do it, just as the Maring did. Culture creates rules that enable us to easily navigate our social and work relationships. It allows us to do this without having to constantly rethink how to do things or renegotiate shared understandings with others. Sometimes, we simply follow the rules without consciously expressing them or even being aware of them. Culture streamlines and simplifies the day-to-day management of our environment, whether it happens to be a forest or an office.

In linguistics, the tendency to simplify concepts by grouping them together is known as "chunking," and the *kaiko* shows how culture is a form of collective chunking. For the Maring, this ritual was a simple way to manage complex interconnections among managing resources, reaffirming community bonds, easing social tension, and practicing spirituality. The *kaiko* became an elegant way to "chunk" all of this work and an invisible part of the tribe's social foundations.

The invisibility helps explain the challenge that culture can pose. It took a dedicated researcher living with the Maring months to understand their motivations and meanings. Rappaport had to work hard to "unchunk" all of the dense interactions and symbolism he was seeing. Now imagine how much more difficult this is when you have days or hours, not months, to create team alignment around a new decision or project, and you have to do it while being in the thick of work rather than standing outside as a detached observer of your team's culture: the patterns of behavior, symbols, and tools used to solve problems.

The upshot is that teams easily become misaligned—often without team members recognizing the problem. They may think they are speaking the same language in the same way, but often when outsiders listen closely to their words and look at their behaviors, they observe a gap between what teams say or think they are doing and what they are actually doing. Teams can also lose touch with their environment—even though they deny it—and thus fail to achieve hoped-for results.

Every team has its own set of rules, because, as we have emphasized, all groups create rules, whether the rules are conscious or not. Human beings have evolved to create collaboration-guiding rules, which have worked fabulously well for centuries. Collaborative behavior has proven to be valuable in nearly every environment, allowing humans to dominate other species that are stronger, bigger, and faster.

The key to this versatility is an ability to make rules and change them when a situation calls for it. Adaptable cultures thrive. Similarly, adaptable teams thrive: they align their rules with the demands of a situation. But things can go way off track when misalignments occur. The result is a saying-doing gap: a disconnect between what a team says it is doing and what it is actually doing.

The Saying-Doing Gap

Our research shows that the saying-doing gap, which can be observed to some degree in virtually every group of people engaged in a collaborative activity, is the most common explanation for poor teamwork. The saying-doing gap develops for two basic reasons. The first occurs when a team is conflicted about its commitments, while the second is related to a team's commitments being out of step with the external environment, such as other parts of an organization or the marketplace. What the two reasons have in common is misalignment with situational factors, caused by a lack of situational awareness (see Figure 2.1).

Figure 2.1   The Three Levels of Situational Awareness

Reason 1: Conflicting Team Commitments

The first kind of problem plagued many of the product teams at Microsoft,[3] ultimately dragging the company down from its position as a market leader in the 1980s and 1990s to an also-ran behind the likes of Apple and Amazon in the 2000s. What accounts for Microsoft's "lost decade," as one journalist called it?

Three Levels of Situational Awareness: Microsoft

The fate of Microsoft's technology unit is a window into the company's larger issues. The team of executives who led the technology unit was seeking to produce long-term innovations that would produce market-making technologies over time. The team had targeted one such innovation when it created an early prototype for an e-reader in 1998, years before the Kindle and the iPad would see the light of day.

After Bill Gates balked at the initial concept, declaring, "I just don't like it," the entire team was moved under the purview of the Office product group, a division structured around the need to constantly crank out new products and updates on a short-term basis. All of a sudden, a team that was supposed to be creating breakthrough technologies on a long time-horizon was plunged into a culture driven by quarterly reporting on profits and losses.

Another cultural misalignment the team faced was one that had affected the organization as a whole: the infamous stack-ranking system. This performance review program, also called "the bell curve," dictated that every manager identify a certain number of top and bottom performers on their teams. No matter if you had 10 all-stars on your team: some of them would have to receive poor reviews. This fostered an overly competitive environment in which teams prioritized their ranking over contributing their best efforts. One engineer described the atmosphere this created: "the behavior this engenders, people do everything they can to stay out of the bottom bucket. . . . People responsible for features will openly sabotage other people's efforts. One of the most valuable things I learned was to give the appearance of being courteous while withholding just enough information from colleagues to ensure they didn't get ahead of me on the rankings."

Team members who were supposed to be focused on building the next breakthrough product were torn. They could collaborate and risk letting someone else get ahead, or hoard their own contributions to avoid being at the bottom of the pile. These conflicting cultural norms created a major gap on the technology team tasked with developing the e-reader. People may have been speaking the language of long-term innovation and collaboration, but in practice they were compelled to seek out quick wins and to engage in destructive competition. Hence, a classic saying-doing gap developed between lofty goals and political infighting.

The e-reader would never come to fruition. Instead, the team released Microsoft Reader software in 1999 that was built to run on a Pocket PC, rather than a larger, touchscreen pad as the team had originally envisioned (and was later popularized by the iPad). Despite having had a big lead on Apple and Amazon, Microsoft Reader was a flop.

The fate of Microsoft's technology team highlights the fact that a team does not exist in a vacuum. It is made up of members who are part of other groups with their own rules that can conflict with the team's commitments. As Geertz says, we are all part of "multiple webs of significance"[4]: different teams, units, and social groups. When the values and expected behaviors change in one group we belong to, it affects how we behave in other groups.

Thus, shared assumptions become misaligned, and how things get done changes in ways that a team leader may not notice. When the Microsoft team was moved into the Office product group, members found themselves beholden to conflicting expectations and values, creating a gap between their goal of innovation and their actual day-to-day work of surviving in a competitive culture with a short time horizon.

Reason 2: Misalignment with the Environment

The second kind of saying-doing gap has its roots in another conflict: being disconnected from the environment surrounding a team. This is a major cause of the well-documented phenomenon known as "groupthink."

Take the case of Ron Johnson,[5] a Steve Jobs acolyte who served as CEO of JC Penney for less than two years before being shown the door. JC Penney had been in decline as the purchasing power of its middle-class customers steadily flagged and online commerce battered its brick and mortar profits.

Three Levels of Situational Awareness: Ron Johnson at JC Penney

When then-CEO Mike Ullman began experiencing health issues, the board took the opportunity to seek out new leadership that could bring a winning strategy and an injection of energy into the business. In Johnson, the board thought they had the savior they were looking for. He had helped to revitalize the Target brand and was the architect of the trendy design and engaging customer experience of Apple's stores. When Johnson and the leadership team he brought from Apple sought to completely transform the company's culture and brand, the board enthusiastically expressed its support.

Johnson called his strategy a "cleanse," but it was more like a demolition. Johnson laid off 19,000 employees and attempted to rid the company of any sign of the old way of doing things. At one point, Johnson's team even installed a cube in the Plano, Texas, office where employees were urged to toss any items that displayed the old logo. Eventually 9,000 pounds of memorabilia from the old JC Penney were collected. Johnson also gave the stores the Apple treatment, bringing in youth-oriented brands, and ending the company's long-standing use of coupons and sales to attract customers, instead promoting a single "fair and square" price on all items.

The strategy was met with initial enthusiasm as the stock price vaulted and employees celebrated the new life Johnson had brought to JC Penney—now called simply JCP. But signs of trouble began to appear. The company began shedding customers, and employees grew disgruntled as Johnson spent lavishly on events celebrating the transformation while laying off thousands.

Despite JCP's declining performance, the executives on Ron Johnson's team maintained an unwavering commitment to the transformation strategy. Most of the new hires declined to move to Plano to be near the company headquarters, and would meet separately in the Ritz Carlton where they all stayed during company visits. Some disdained the long-time executives, with one reportedly referring to them as Dumb Old Penney Employees (DOPEs). The DOPEs, not to be outdone, called the new group of Johnson-ites the Bad Apples.

They resented the divisiveness of the newcomers, as one commented: "You felt like you were back in high school with the cool kids and the non-cool kids." Johnson preferred to fire the dissenters instead of seeking to address warning signs. There was no place for devil's advocates on the road to JCP's salvation: "I choose to inspire and create believers," he told one reporter. "I don't like negativity. Skepticism takes the oxygen out of innovation."

The insularity of Johnson's team prevented them from seeing that the aspects of their culture that had worked for Apple—the startup mentality, the trendy image, the visionary bravado—were seriously misaligned with the JC Penney environment. The loss of customers and revenue turned out to be not a transition period but a longer decline. Ron Johnson was eventually replaced—just a year and a half after implementation of his strategy had begun—by none other than the old CEO, Ullman. JCP, re-renamed JC Penney, reversed course and reestablished many of the practices from before Johnson's tenure.

The downfall of the "Bad Apples" demonstrates another critical aspect of culture for managing teams: the rules that govern a group's behaviors will often carry on long after their original reason for being has vanished and even when the rules become counterproductive.

Rice or Wheat People?   To illustrate this point about the surprising persistence of rules, consider the following question: Are you a "wheat" person or a "rice" person? You probably have never thought of yourself in such terms. But a widely discussed study shows[6] that the staple crops your ancestors cultivated shape your everyday behaviors in unexpected ways. East Asians often value group harmony and fitting in with others while Northern Europeans lean toward individualism and standing out in a crowd. The study's authors explain that the culture in each of those regions is rooted in agricultural practices related to growing rice and wheat.

One crop relies heavily on collaboration across fields for proper irrigation whereas the other requires much less coordination among farmers. The influence of these working styles has become pervasive in the East and the West. Even Northern Europeans who have not had agriculture in their family for generations tend to behave like "wheat people." The deeply ingrained rules of a particular culture can persist in ways no one is even aware of. As we said before, familiarity equals invisibility.

While a strong culture can bind a people together in positive ways, it can also cause disconnects in new situations in which old rules are a poor fit. Johnson and his team ran into this problem when they tried to import the Apple culture into one of the oldest department stores in the country. The "Apple people" were out of sync with the "JC Penney people" in some obvious ways but also in some unnoticed ways that derailed Johnson's transformation program.

Check Alignment: Revealing the Gap between Saying and Doing

Both the Microsoft and JCP teams had a hard time dealing with situational factors that caused a gap between saying and doing. The e-reader developers were caught between conflicting commitments to short-term results and longer-term product innovation, while Ron Johnson's team was out of touch with the dominant cultural environment. These classic disconnects are hard to see when your team is focused on just getting its work done.

So, how can you reveal saying-doing gaps and keep your team aligned with its internal commitments as well as its external environment? To bridge the gaps, you have to view yourselves as outsiders would, as though you were an exotic tribe like the Maring. True, this is a tall order. But others have learned how to do it, applying a tried and true method of qualitative research: participant observation. We can teach you how to use it.

The Stud Gun Accident

Let's see how useful this method was in an incident that one of our fellow business anthropologists, Tracy Meerwath, observed.

It started with a minor accident at a General Motors manufacturing plant[7] in Lansing, Michigan: a robotic stud gun had broken from its air pipe and smashed on the ground, scattering parts and stud pellets all over the factory floor. Ned, an electrician, had determined that it would be unsafe to try to use a backup stud gun and assessed that the assembly line would have to be shut down. His supervisor Al stormed over. Without consulting Ned, Al ordered him to get the backup gun running, exclaiming: "Bypass it! We are in the business of making cars." Ned angrily retorted that Al didn't understand the problem. Al ignored him, leaving Ned to spend the rest of the day getting the backup working and the original stud gun fixed as he muttered about the low standard of safety at the plant.

It was a simple interaction, but like a prism it also reflected the multiple cultural conflicts inhibiting performance at the plant. Al and Ned's team had been charged with engaging in more collaborative behavior as part of a larger change initiative within GM as the company attempted to move away from its traditionally siloed culture. It was a team goal, but it was one that Al violated for good reason. As indicated by his declaration about the "business of making cars," Al knew that GM cared about productivity and cost reduction as much as if not more than collaboration and safety. He felt pressured to get the line moving as quickly as possible.

For his part, Ned's angry response was driven by Al's negation of his expertise, further exacerbated by the fact that, unlike the union worker Ned, Al was hired as his supervisor on a contract basis. Ned saw Al's temporary hiring as proof that safety and quality control were not the company's real priorities. As he would later say, "Quality talk is just that—talk. The real priority is jobs off the end of the line."

The combination of all of these factors led to an encounter that completely undermined the values of collaboration the team was supposed to be following. In other words, this was a major saying-doing gap.

Notice how many tensions and conflicting priorities were packed into the exchange: conflicting team and organizational goals exaggerated Ned and Al's personal differences as members of the unionized labor force and management. But the work continued. Al went on with his day, Ned set up the stud gun, and the plant kept humming. It is exactly in these seemingly mundane interactions that crucial team misalignments play out.

Later, when workers and management at the plant took the time to unpack all of the conflicting rules, they turned the incident into a case study that they used to facilitate dialogues about barriers to collaboration within the organization. It even became the basis of training software that other teams throughout GM used to effectively diagnose and address their own collaboration issues.

Bottom line: the workers and managers at the GM plant *became their own observers*.

Learning to Become Your Own Observer

To find and close the deep disconnects embedded in this mundane interaction, the GM workers and managers needed to perform three tasks:

1. They had to *adopt an observer's mindset* to view their own behavior the way others would see it.
2. They had to *collect data about situational factors* that produce rule conflicts.
3. Finally, they had to *create a psychologically safe space* for problem solving.

HPTs work hard to become their own observers, because cultural drift is inevitable. No matter how much work you put into establishing the right commitments, circumstances will change and personal priorities will evolve in ways that invalidate or clash with some of the commitments initially established on your team. Thus, you need to regularly check alignment.

Adopt an Observer's Mindset

To be able to identify the underlying misalignments on your team, you have to reduce the biases that distort your judgment and cause you to miss important cues. Without this observer's mindset, you will have a hard time diagnosing team problems, no matter how much information you have at your disposal. As an illustration, consider another conflict between competing priorities that occurred at GM.[8] This one had tragic consequences.

It all started with a fatal decision made by Raymond, a GM engineer. Beginning in 2002, Raymond started receiving a batch of faulty ignition switches from a supplier that turned to the "off" position far too easily when jostled. When he found it would be costly to fix the switches, he decided to ignore the issue and allowed production to continue. It wasn't until 2005 that he decided to have the supplier reengineer the switches, quietly ordering the improved part without changing their identification number in his logs. By then, the damage was done and over the next decade, 50 fatalities would result from the faulty switches as they suddenly flipped off at high speeds, shutting down anti-lock breaks and airbags.

Federal investigations finally led to GM's fixing the ignition issue. By that time, 2.6 million vehicles had been recalled and over $900 million in fines and damages had been paid. Why were the warning signs ignored until the faulty switches became a catastrophic problem?

As one analyst described it, General Motors "was a company that … was always dominated by bean counters, and bean counters had only one objective and that is make the numbers, at all cost." This intensive focus on costs permeated the culture of the company, creating a bias that blinded higher-ups to critical information indicating that the faulty switches could prove to be ethically and financially disastrous.

One whistleblower recounted going from supervisor to supervisor with his concerns, only to be told that a recall would be impractical and cost-prohibitive. Numerous people at GM had the information they needed to act, but their biases prevented them from seeing the underlying misalignment between competing priorities: cost-cutting and vehicle safety.

How can you ensure you don't miss the critical cues about conflicts hiding in your own team's interactions? One powerful solution is to bring in an outside observer—one who is unfamiliar with your group's particular dynamics and rules. Recall how Rappaport was able to discover the resource scarcity driving pig sacrifices among the Maring tribe that he studied. The phenomenon he witnessed was hiding in plain sight, but it was so familiar to the Maring that they never noticed it. It took an outside observer to recognize a behavioral rule that no one else saw.

Tracy Meerwath and her team played a similar role as anthropologists at GM. Being removed from Ned and Al's team, they were able to identify a tension between collaboration and autonomy that Ned and Al likely did not recognize on their own. Outside observers like Meerwath, whether they are consultants or just a colleague from another division, can be invaluable in helping you see the obvious misalignments on your team.

Become "Outsider Insiders"

What if you can't bring in an outsider? You can become an "outsider insider" by paying attention to two common conceptual biases that can blind you to the impact of your own behaviors.

Two key biases that lead to misalignment
Overvaluing Outcomes
Reassess processes even when you are successful.
Motivated Blindness
Seek out disconfirming evidence.

One of those biases leads to "overvaluing outcomes." As Harvard professor Max Bazerman has shown,[9] when a process results in a favorable outcome, we tend to ignore the mistakes or tensions that could cause problems in other situations. For example, one study shows that NBA coaches are more likely to revisit their strategy after a loss than after a win, even if the win was a close call. In general, when things are going smoothly, we tend to be highly selective in noticing what is working and what needs to be changed. To overcome this bias when reviewing past decisions and actions on your team, even if you achieved desired outcomes, get in the habit of imagining what would have happened if a situation had taken a turn for the worse and how your team would have responded to the resulting problems. Be careful to note how behaviors that produced success could have led, under different circumstances, to serious problems.

Another common bias goes by the name of "motivated blindness."[10] In the famous words of Upton Sinclair: "It is difficult to get a man[11] to understand something, when his salary depends on his not understanding it." This was undoubtedly the case for many of the GM managers who failed to take action on the faulty ignition switch. But financial concerns are not the only interest that motivates blindness. It could be that a team member who is causing problems happens to be a good friend, or that you have an aversion to bringing up difficult issues with your team.

To reduce the effects of this bias, management scholars Soyer and Hogarth[12] recommend creating a habit of explicitly seeking out disconfirming evidence. When you find yourself making assumptions about the nature of a team problem, ask: What would convince me that my interpretation is wrong? Actively seek out evidence that disproves your beliefs to ensure you are not letting your own preferences and interests cloud your judgment.

Situational Factors That Produce Conflicts: The Power of Systematic Data-Gathering

Once you have created the observer's mindset, you should systematically gather data that helps anticipate potential situational conflicts that will sap your team's engagement and hurt performance. At the GM plant, for example, the safety-oriented rules that Ned was expected to abide by were likely to come into conflict with the production-driving rules that Al needed to follow. In your own team environment, you can anticipate conflicts by looking for the sources of similar tensions on three levels: interpersonal, team, and environment.

At the interpersonal level, you can take the temperature of your team's engagement with a simple set of statements that can quickly be rated (see Figure 2.2). The responses will give you an initial sense of whether team members might be feeling alienated from the group and why. Team members should anonymously rate these statements on a scale of 1 (strongly disagree) to 5 (strongly agree). It is a quick and easy way to uncover misalignment issues at the interpersonal level that need to be raised.

At the team level, you have to pay attention to your own teams' rules the way anthropologist Roy Rappaport observed the Marings' *kaiko* ritual. As Isaac Newton once said: "If I have ever made any valuable discoveries, it has been owing more to patient observation than to any other reason." The problem, as we have said, is that familiarity equals invisibility. So how do you make familiar but potentially conflict-producing rules visible?

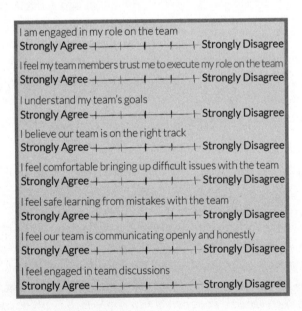

Figure 2.2   Team Temperature Survey

Recall that, in the initial team commitment chartering discussions, your team identified major priorities within the multiple groups to which each person belongs: other teams, families, community organizations, and so on. Revisiting these potentially competing priorities can help you become aware of rule-conflict hotspots that could flare up on your team.

You can use the Misalignments Worksheet in the Resources section to identify specific misalignments and begin to understand why they may be occurring. This gives you concrete, observable insights that your team can discuss and act upon.

In the left column of your team's worksheet, you list the commitments you initially created in the chartering process, and in the center column, note actually observed behaviors that go against the commitments. This commitments checklist can help you become aware of unnoticed behaviors that might contradict the rules you initially created when you established team commitments.

At the *environmental level,* you can begin to dissect *why* conflicts and misalignments have emerged by looking at factors outside the team. For each of the conflicts you identified, you should ask the following questions:

- Are your team members' personal commitments outside of work causing conflicts with their team commitments?

- Are the other teams in the organization your members are a part of affecting their contribution to this team, because of looming deadlines or other issues?

- Has there been a shift in organizational priorities that led to this conflict, such as new projects, initiatives, policies, or systems?

- Has anything changed in the market that is affecting your project, such as customer trends, new legislation, or technological developments?

Enter these potential reasons in the right column on your Misalignments Worksheet. They are assumptions to be tested when you meet with the team.

Create the Space for Problem Solving: Psychological Safety

Once you have identified potential or actual sources of team conflicts, the next step is to have an open discussion about them. That *sounds* good, but Jon Krakauer will tell you[13] it is not so easy.

A writer for *Outside* magazine, Krakauer joined an expedition to the summit of Everest that would end in one of the worst tragedies in the history of the legendary mountain. It was the spring of 1996 when he agreed to join Rob Hall, one of the world's best climbers, on a trip organized through Hall's adventure travel company.

The group included some relative novices, but Hall was confident in his ability to get the team to the summit and back safely. Hall laid down clear goals and a timeline for reaching the summit. He established roles by assigning trained guides and Sherpas to specific duties and determining where in the group they would be during the climb. He set rigid norms about communication and the chain of command, telling his clients: "I will tolerate no dissension up there. My word will be absolute law, beyond appeal. If you don't like a particular decision I make, I'd be happy to discuss it with you afterward, but not while we're up on the hill."

Members of the expedition seemed to be in agreement on the ground rules. As they began their ascent on May 6, Hall felt good about the cohesion of the team. Yet while the clients appeared unified on the surface, some quietly expressed apprehension about the lack of training and low level of preparedness among some members in the group. Krakauer would later write: "We were a team in name only, I'd sadly come to realize. Although in a few hours we would leave camp as a group, we would ascend as individuals, linked to one another by neither rope nor any deep sense of loyalty. Each client was in it for himself or herself, pretty much."

This gap between the apparent cohesion of the group and the every-man-for-himself attitude held privately by many of the climbers came back to haunt the expedition when it met adversity on the way up the mountain. As the weather worsened and some of the climbers began to struggle, things fell apart. The lead Sherpa, who was supposed to lay down ropes on the most dangerous parts of the trail, had dropped far back, helping to tow one of the group's ailing members. The delays caused the team to fall behind schedule, but it pushed on regardless.

On the descent, the wind began to howl and snow lashed the mountain. Many climbers barely made it back to their encampment, and those who did woke to find that Hall and several others had lost their lives. At the heart of the breakdown was the fact that no one felt comfortable speaking up when the team was clearly contradicting its own rules.

Setting the Stage: Build Trust and Rapport

The fateful Everest expedition shows that, before teams can solve problems, they have to create a space for giving and receiving honest feedback: the final step in checking alignment. Teammates should feel that they can speak up about issues, admit mistakes, and ask for help without being shamed or penalized by the group. Amy Edmondson calls this "psychological safety."[14] Her research demonstrates that teams with this characteristic communicate more openly, share information more freely, and ultimately make better decisions.

In fact, many studies suggest that open communication is more important to teams than intelligence. For example, in one influential experiment, groups with high collective IQ[15] underperformed on exercises that involve brainstorming, problem solving, and moral reasoning. Higher-performing groups had three things in common: (1) Inclusive group dialogue; (2) High emotional intelligence (EI), and (3) A greater number of women (who score higher than men on EI assessments). In a team setting, communication and interpersonal understanding frequently trump smarts.

Sadly, in a business context, teams often refrain from engaging in open, inclusive dialogue because they have good reasons not to. This problem came into stark relief during a workshop we led for a global retail company—call it Global Brands International—that was focused on revamping its business model. A team of senior executives was charged with developing an e-commerce strategy. After a day spent discussing this challenge, the team concluded that the real issue was much bigger than the one they had been asked to consider. The company owned a portfolio of high-end and budget brands, and the team was stumped over how they could begin to establish a stronger online presence without having a comprehensive brand identity to go along with it. As one of the team members described the issue: "It's like pulling a thread in one part of a sweater and seeing the whole garment come apart." Although this was an important insight, the team members felt it was risky to share it with the CEO. After some debate, however, they decided to tell him about it in a scheduled presentation.

The CEO joined the presentation by phone. His voice boomed through the room's overhead speakers, swirling around the team members like a powerful spirit. Even so, the discussion went well until the branding issue came up. "We need a process check," roared the voice of the CEO, sounding like a proclamation from a burning bush. The "process check" turned into a rebuke, as he proceeded to scold the team for going beyond the scope of its assigned task. After a brief silence, the team returned to the presentation, avoiding further mention of branding.

When team members lack psychological safety, they stop speaking their minds on important issues. This is a costly limitation. When teams feel safe, they can take full advantage of diverse perspectives freely expressed, anticipate difficult challenges, and find solutions that no one person would have discovered on their own. But fostering psychological safety requires much more than exhorting team members to "take risks" and "be honest" and "deliver."

Like any social group, teams are constantly involved in a negotiation over what it means to be a member. Individuals participate in an endless give-and-take around what their membership entails, what sacrifices they must make to remain a member in good standing, and what they can expect in return.

As sociologist Howard Becker showed in his classic study *Outsiders*,[16] people make choices every day about whether to remain in a group or exit to pursue other opportunities. A jazz musician, for example, must decide whether to be a "true artist" and play for small crowds of aficionados or go commercial and join the "squares" who frequent larger venues. Anyone who joins a team faces similar choices about where to spend his or her energy. Should it be channeled toward the collective goals of the team, toward self-interested commitments, or even toward self-preservation? Team leaders often find themselves in the position of having to influence or even bargain over such choices. In a wide review of studies on leadership qualities, Robert Hogan, the creator of the popular personality assessment,[17] finds that a leader's fundamental role throughout human history has been "persuading people to set aside, for a time, their selfish pursuits and work in support of the communal interest."

This is a never-ending process because individual interests are constantly shifting. What separates HPTs from low-performing teams is not that they somehow sidestep these conflicts. HPTs accept and channel conflict to the betterment of the group. George Kohlrieser, a well-known hostage negotiator and co-author of *Care to Dare,*[18] has shown that, contrary to the popular notion that you can separate "business decisions" from personal relations, leadership is always intensely personal. To be effective, teams have to excel at building trust, encouraging honesty and risk-taking, and making others feel comfortable expressing disagreement.

All sound advice. But many people have personalities that make it difficult to create these conditions. Even if you are more of an agreeable Paul McCartney than a confrontational John Lennon or a "burning bush" CEO, it is easy to revert to defensiveness or even aggression during times of stress. For example, we worked with a president of a major manufacturing company who organized a team of a hand-picked executives he described disturbingly as a "radical sect." This sect terrorized people on other teams even as the president urged all of the company's employees to collaborate across organizational boundaries. Once again, the saying-doing gap made it difficult to align with a group's stated values.

So, how do you foster psychological safety so that, when it is time to have difficult conversations, team members will be collaborative, supportive, and open?

Build Individual Relationships with One-on-Ones   Rock musicians need psychological safety just as much as business people.

Management scholar Christopher Roussin[19] made this discovery when he consulted to a fractious band on the verge of breaking up. Roussin also learned that the most important way to create an atmosphere of psychological safety is to have frequent one-on-one conversations.

Roussin was contacted by the band-leader, Winona, who was struggling after one of her musicians, Sean, abruptly announced he was burned out and needed to take some time off. Wanting to keep up a busy tour schedule, she asked her friend Rod to temporarily replace Sean. The result was a near mutiny by the four other members, who resented Rod's presence. Winona described the subsequent summer rehearsals and shows as an experience of "extended torture." The situation came to a head when one of the band members wrote a nasty email to Winona about just how dysfunctional the band had become.

Tips for One-on-Ones
Listen and Inquire
Ask questions.
Listen carefully.
Avoid reacting.
Show Humility
Ask for feedback on what you can do better.
Accept criticism.
Solicit advice on changing your behavior.
Discuss Styles
Know your default style.
Ask yourself which style would work best in this conversation and adapt.

Roussin suggested Winona have one-on-one conversations with each team member. Knowing that nonjudgmental listening has been shown to create psychological safety, Roussin coached Winona to avoid becoming reactive and simply listen. And indeed, band members quickly opened up during these conversations. Winona learned that Sean wanted to spend more time with his fiancée. He felt the group was doing too many shows away from home, but he felt unable to bring up the issue with Winona due to her "overly harsh" style. To her surprise, other band members expressed similar feelings.

At the end of the summer when Sean rejoined the group, Winona led an open discussion with the band. Everyone agreed to do fewer shows and stay close to home to prevent burn-out. Even more, the band took a big step toward becoming an HPT. Winona exclaimed to Roussin: "People are picking up the phone now if something isn't clear or if something rubs them the wrong way. And personally, if something comes up in the future, I feel a lot more equipped now to handle it."

Winona was able to create an atmosphere of trust and support that enabled band members to have tough conversations about changes to their routine. Of course, this was far from easy. It took a lot of face time before team members could even talk openly. Creating genuine rapport and trust on your team takes work—more work than just declaring, "There are no wrong answers." But taking the time for one-on-one conversations usually leads to a valuable outcome: a feeling that you are willing to walk the talk when it comes to hearing people out.

Discuss Bargaining Styles   Since team discussions often involve negotiation, we recommend taking account of individual bargaining styles to ensure that as a group you communicate in the most effective way. Our colleague Richard Shell's Bargaining Styles Assessment,[20] which you can find in *Bargaining for Advantage,* is a useful starting point for getting a sense of each person's preferred approach:

- *Competitors* tend to be direct, firm, and forceful. Forcefulness is good, as long as others feel they can express their perspectives.
- *Collaborators* are curious, probing, and supportive. They aim to find creative solutions to complex problems that address the underlying needs of all team members. Collaborators may spend

too much time probing, however, and not enough on actually
making a decision.

- *Compromisers* are brisk, efficient, and quick. They have a tendency
  to aim for 50/50-type solutions that appeal to everyone. The dark
  side of the compromising is impatience, which can lead to closing
  off dialogue before enough options have been considered.

- *Accommodators* are sensitive, empathetic, and flexible. They are
  focused on keeping the peace, even at the expense of giving up
  their own position to attain it.

- *Avoiders* are diplomatic, outwardly calm, and indirect. They
  would rather sidestep the push and pull of negotiating altogether.
  Avoiders may struggle with bringing up issues that need discussion.

By having your team members take the assessment and discuss
their bargaining styles, you can shape conversations to ensure everyone
has a voice. For example, the avoiders on your team are more likely
to speak up if they are given the role of facilitator. They will feel
comfortable contributing because they know that they are not only
encouraged but expected to note the dysfunctional dynamics that
others may be feeling but are hesitant to talk about.

Using one-on-ones to discuss bargaining styles and clarify informal
roles will help you develop strategies for having productive discussions
and encouraging team members to disagree constructively.

Minding the Gaps

How can you take the next step and turn your own band of misfits into
rock stars, as Winona did? In this chapter, we have shown you how
you can identify hard-to-see problems and create an environment that
prepares your team for problem solving. From time to time, you will
need to have difficult conversations about changing behaviors. The
problem is that identifying this need and actually addressing it are two
different things, for all the reasons we have discussed up to this point.

No team can completely eliminate tensions or conflicts. But HPTs use tools to frame the right questions and find the answers that improve alignment with their own group culture and the environment. At the heart of checking alignment is the process of cultivating an observer's mindset. This involves collecting data about conflict-producing situational factors, creating the sense of psychological safety needed for problem solving, and closing the gaps between aspirations and actions. In the next chapter, we show you how to make the behavioral changes needed to close these saying-doing gaps.

HPT Takeaways

Conflicting commitments create saying-doing gaps

Gaps form when commitments come into conflict or fall out of alignment with situational factors.

Create an "observer's mindset"

By neutralizing common conceptual biases, you can more easily observe potential and actual sources of conflict on and around your team.

Assess situational factors

You can learn to collect data about conflict-producing situational factors at the individual, team, and environmental levels.

Cultivate psychological safety

Have one-on-one discussions to create a space for reflection and open the possibility for change within the team.

3 Close: To Bridge the Saying-Doing Gap, Act Like a STAR

They thought he had lost his mind. The business was teetering on the brink of bankruptcy, but the CEO had latched onto a decidedly nonstrategic topic: workplace safety. No one could possibly say it was unimportant, but concerned investors wanted to hear details about markets, revenues, and profit. Where was the business plan?

An analyst asked about finance metrics. Nothing doing. "I'm not certain you heard me," the CEO answered. "If you want to understand how Alcoa is doing, you need to look at our workplace safety figures."

You might recognize the speaker as Paul O'Neill, who merits a whole chapter in Charles Duhigg's *The Power of Habit: Why We Do What We Do in Life and Business*.[1] O'Neill used that power to engineer an amazing turnaround. A year after he gave his unexpected lecture about workplace safety to a group of dismayed shareholders and industry observers, company performance had rebounded and profits had reached record highs.

In bringing Alcoa back from the precipice, O'Neill pursued a strategy embraced by successful managers and team leaders to close the gap between aspirations and action: he *got specific*. He avoided the all-too-common CEO "cheerleading," as he put it dismissively, and focused on just one concrete thing. Research on positive behavioral change has confirmed the efficacy of pinpointing measurable actions and monitoring small, step-by-step improvements. For example, would-be fitness fanatics rarely stick with their workout plan if they target an abstract goal like: "Get in shape." They do much better when they set concrete milestones, such as: "Go to the gym three times by next Friday." What works for individuals works for teams and organizations, as O'Neill demonstrated in dramatically improving Alcoa's operations.

Getting specific is the key to closing the saying-doing gaps that you identified using the tools we introduced in the previous chapter. Once you have observed misalignments and set the stage for having productive discussions about them, you can work with your team on getting committed again. Elite athletes close the gap by getting specific, and so do artists, scientists, and managers. Specificity is the key to acting like a STAR, a process we explain in this chapter.

Swimming in the Deep Water

Like Paul O'Neill, high-performing team members avoid cheerleading when they are giving each other feedback. They identify specific behaviors that help or hinder performance and suggest ways to implement or enhance them. For example, an EDP participant named Adedayo noted after some reflection that he expressed his ideas like a "machine gun" in team meetings, spraying his words indiscriminately around a conversation and killing his group's creativity. At the end of a decision-making session, his teammates told him to talk 75 percent less the next time. The definite target helped Adedayo calibrate his contributions and gave others an opportunity to bring their proposals out into the open. By getting specific, the team narrowed the saying-doing gap between a high-level commitment to out-of-the-box thinking and the way group discussions had actually been going.

In this sense, HPTs engage in "deep" versus "shallow" discussions about goals, norms, and behaviors.[2] We borrow this distinction from University of California anthropologist Mica Pollock, who has shown that abstractions rarely capture the reality of how groups and organizations operate. In the early stages of commitment-setting, HPTs may start by discussing intangible goals like "winning," "greatness," and "creativity," but their attention later turns to particulars like the amount of time spent on a topic or the number and kind of comments made by a team member. (Think Adedayo the machine-gunner.) As HPTs develop, they swim from the conversational "shallows" into the "deep waters" of specific feedback. HPTs navigate these waters by acting like STARs—a process that starts with getting specific and includes using behavioral prompts.

It takes work to move into the deep water. A poignant scene in the acclaimed film *Boyhood* illustrates the difficulty. Ethan Hawke's character Mason Sr. is driving his son and daughter home from school after having been away. As we have all done countless times in small-talk conversation with our loved ones, Mason Sr. asks the kids a mind-numbing, general question: "How was your week?"

The younger Mason and Samantha offer the typical adolescent responses like "fine" and "pretty good." Suddenly seeing this moment as a sign of growing distance between himself and his children, Mason Sr. pulls over the car and demands they engage him with more seriousness.

"Dad," Samantha retorts, "these questions are hard to answer … they are too abstract."

The son interjects, "What about you, Dad? How was your week?"

Mason Sr. pauses for a moment and admits, "I see your point."

When it comes time to discuss team problems, we tend to make statements like, "Let's talk about the issues," and remind team members, "There are no wrong answers," and urge them to "Check egos at the door." Like the question "How was your week?" these pronouncements get at the right idea but fail to create the space for people to actually reflect and respond honestly. They are just too abstract.

Situational Awareness: Ambitious Goals Are Not Enough

On May 25, 1961, John F. Kennedy announced to a joint session of Congress[3] that the United States "should commit itself to achieving the goal, before this decade is out, of landing a man on the moon and returning him safely to the earth." His words rank as one of the most visionary appeals in recorded history and are often cited as a model for leaders of motivational rhetoric.

The months of careful preparation that preceded JFK's address typically receive far less attention, but we think they constitute the heart of the real story. For it is the preparation that ultimately made the stirring lunar-inspired words so powerful and memorable, even though they accounted for just a fifth of the famous speech that also addressed several other urgent policy challenges such as a badly flagging economy and national security. Facing plenty of sublunary problems that would have stressed even the most capable executive team, the president and his advisors were willing to go public with the audacious moonshot goal because they had already won support for it behind the scenes from influential politicians, scientists, economists, and government administrators.

Before his election as president, Kennedy displayed little interest in space exploration, and he delegated the responsibility for the lunar landing issue to Vice-President Lyndon Johnson, who was deftly positioning the space program with key senators such as Robert Kerr, chairman of the Space Committee. Kerr made no bones about serving parochial interests, including his own. He openly admitted, "I represent myself first, the state of Oklahoma second, and the people of the United States third, and don't you forget it!"

Johnson therefore made sure Kerr knew that he and his con-stituencies would benefit from massive investments in the technology required to send astronauts on a round trip to the moon. Kerr then played an important part in selecting the new head of the National Aeronautics and Space Administration (NASA): James E. Webb. Despite his initial doubts about the moon mission, Webb had the right mix of political skill, energy, and charisma to advocate for JFK's agenda with law-makers and military brass.

Bottom line: By the time the president made the historic address to Congress, he could bank on critical support from a host of well-placed people he needed to realize his goal. Walter A. McDougall,

the level-headed historian[4] who wrote the definitive account of
the Apollo years, put the point as baldly as possible. All the major
figures—Kennedy, Johnson, Webb, Kerr, and many others—"saw ways
in which an accelerated space program could help them solve problems
in their own shop or serve their own interests." Because JFK was in
touch with the practical reality of his situation and had aligned a whole
team behind his vision, he felt comfortable making a strong case for
the lunar program.

Since gaps easily develop between reality and ambitious goals,
HPTs are always working to maintain situational awareness and
fine-tune both their ambitions and actions accordingly. The way
Kennedy and his team positioned the Apollo program is a historic
success story in this regard. But another story, about the tragic events
that overtook the Granite Mountain Interagency Hotshot Crew,
shows how hard it can be to balance goals against a complex and
ever-changing situation.

The Hotshot crew was an elite team if ever there was one. In every
part of the United States, the crew fought wildfires that had become
raging, rolling infernos that threatened flora, fauna, and all things
human. Eric March led the Granite Mountain hotshots, and he did
everything right in creating the conditions for peak performance. He
set goals—you can even call them transcendent goals—memorialized
in a dramatic manifesto:[5] "Why do we want to be away from home so
much, work such long hours, risk our lives, and sleep on the ground
100 nights a year? Simply, it's the most fulfilling thing any of us have
ever done. We are not nameless or faceless. We are not expendable. We
are not satisfied with mediocrity, we are not willing to accept being
average. We are not quitters."

March handpicked his team, probing each recruit to determine if
he had the necessary skills and character. Character was paramount,
because the team had to be committed to truth-telling. "When was
the last time you lied," Marsh asked every interviewee. Once selected,
teammates knew exactly how they fit into the crew. Finally, the team
had clear norms that everybody had signed off on. The norms were
based on meticulous analyses of fatal fires and included the safety

system called LCES: Lookouts, Communications, Escape Routes, and Safety Zones. Training drilled the LCES protocol into the crew.

You might conclude that the Hotshot crew was the perfect team: goals, roles, and norms—the key HPT success factors—were all founded on a commitment to truth-telling. No one would use the word "perfect," however, to describe the outcome of the Hotshot Crew's engagement with a fire that bore down on Yarnell, Arizona, in June of 2013. Just the opposite: A heartbreaking scenario unfolded that claimed the lives of 19 elite firefighters.

What happened?

Though the full answer is obviously complicated, the Industrial Commission of Arizona reached a striking conclusion: the Arizona Forestry Division had "implemented suppression strategies that prioritized protection of non-defensible structures and pastureland over firefighter safety." The bureaucratic language obscures an insight articulated by one of the firefighters who survived the blaze. "They wanted to reengage," said Darrell Willis of his comrades who lost their lives. "Sure, they could sit up there in the black [i.e., a safety zone, protected from the encroaching conflagration]. But if they could try to get back into the game, they were going to." In other words, following the LCES protocol, the Hotshots had retreated to a safety zone, but then left it to continue battling the flames.

To put it bluntly: *the Hotshots did precisely what they should not have done*. As Willis reported, "We said we're never going to let this happen to us. It was kind of like a commitment: we can't let this happen to us." But happen it did, because they made a decision that was obviously flawed, in terms of their own protocol and manifesto.

Long story short, situational factors overwhelmed the Hotshots. One of the most important factors was that they were exhausted. A hiker who encountered the firefighters on the way to their final stand took a photograph that captured a disturbing fact. Men trudged uphill in 90-plus degree temperatures, lugging heavy tools and backpacks, their visibly strained faces dripping with sweat. The walls of the Hotshot headquarters where the Hotshots started the day were covered with posters that emphasized the basics: "Don't Let Wildland Urban Interface change your Situational Awareness. Your life is more important than any structure!" If you are rested and calm, this exhortation is blindingly obvious. It is anything but obvious when you are stressed, tapped out, and facing a roaring inferno.

This helps explain why HPTs rely on checklists and prompts: simple reminders to perform the most basic actions in the right way, even as intense situational pressures are making it hard to pay attention to details. In the abstract, high-performing teamwork seems to be based on the science of the blindingly obvious (commit to shared inspirational goals, communicate clearly, support decisions reached by the group, etc., etc.). In reality, however, it is just very hard to remember what to do under the conditions in which most people do their work every day: surrounded by raging fire, on the battlefield, in a cockpit or operating room, even in a conference room facing down a deadline and worried about looking bad.

High-performing teamwork is based on the interactive process of cultivating an ability to notice and respond to the seemingly insignificant details that matter most to closing gaps between goals and action. The process underlies successful firefighting, surgery, office work, parenting—indeed, any activity that requires working with and through others to reach a specified outcome.

ACT LIKE A STAR

Our field research has shown that HPTs create the conditions for peak performance by acting like "STAR"s.

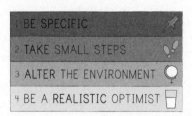

The four STAR steps are the key to closing the saying-doing gap. Each step has its own guidelines, which HPTs adapt to suit their unique circumstances. We explain this model below, and provide you with a condensed version in the Resources section.

1. Be Specific

In order to make improvements, teams need to be hyper-specific about the changes they want to make. This can be tough. Just ask the Apple engineers who endured the brutality of Steve Jobs's special kind of feedback. Andy Grignon, one of the architects of the original iPhone[6] and a member of the team that brought it to market, remembers how Jobs would express his displeasure if your actions failed to measure up to his expectations.

"He just looked at you," Grignon reports, "and very directly said in a very loud and stern voice, 'You are f---ing up my company,' or, 'If we fail, it will be because of you.' He was just very intense. And you would always feel an inch tall [when he was done chewing you out]." While we do not recommend you deliver feedback in the same way, it worked for Jobs because everyone had signed on to the goal of creating an "insanely great" product and was comfortable enough to look past the abuse and see exactly what needed to be done differently.

With all due respect to Steve Jobs, you need not cut your team members down to build them up. You can encourage them to change while you deepen feelings of openness and trust. But you do need to go from shallow to deep with your feedback if you expect team members to take action.

A powerful tool for helping your team drill down into specific changes is the Start/Stop/Continue exercise. It unfolds in simple steps:

- Divide a flipchart or white board into three vertical sections.
- Ask team members to write on individual Post-it notes the specific action they want to start doing, detrimental behaviors they think the team should stop, or positive practices the team should continue.
- Place each Post-it in its proper place on the board.
- Review the postings to see whether there are common themes and consider collectively what you want to change or encourage in the group dynamic.

Start/Stop/Continue is an easy and effective way to spur reflection and develop a behavior-change mindset. It helps you brainstorm ideas for change in an inclusive way that helps you visualize end goals. Try it in your next meeting as a way to get specific about your options for closing the saying-doing gap on your team.

To test whether you have gotten specific enough in this exercise, use visualization and measurement. If you would be unable to *see* a teammate acting on the feedback and *count* the number of times he or she does, then you should work on making your comments more concrete.

Amy Edmondson tells the story of [9] a top management team that was working to develop a new corporate strategy. The situation was urgent and called for specific, actionable steps toward change. But you would not have known it from the conversation. The team consistently spoke in abstract metaphors, such as the popular ship analogy that is all too familiar to anyone who has been involved in a change initiative:

> Listening to Bob talk about the ship, I'd like to explore the difference between the metaphor of the ship and how the rudder gets turned and when, in contrast to a flotilla, where there's lots of little rudders and we're trying to orchestrate the flotilla. I think this contrast is important. At one level, we talk about this ship and all the complexities of trying to determine not only its direction but also how to operationalize the ship in total to get to a certain place, versus allowing a certain degree of freedom that the flotilla analogy evokes.

If you are feeling lost at sea, you are not alone. The team was still adrift six months later as they struggled to turn their abstract conversations about strategy into concrete action.

Applying the *see* and *count* test will tell you

Be Specific

Say This	Not That
Please do not interrupt me, and please repeat my point before responding it.	You need to listen better.
Give me a daily update on your progress.	Meet your deadlines.
To give the other nine people in the group space to talk, limit your talking time to 10 percent of the meeting.	Stop dominating meetings.

whether your feedback goes deep enough. For example, consider the difference between saying, "I want you to listen to me," and, "The next time we have a conversation, I want you to wait three seconds before you respond to me and restate my point before you make another one." The second statement defines what you mean by "listening," while the first is way too abstract.

2. Resolve to Take Small Steps Toward Improving

Let's continue with the example of listening. If you agreed to wait and restate a teammate's words before making another point, you would have resolved to make a small step toward improving communication. Top performers improve by making small steps, and so do HPTs.

Consider the career of Steve Martin,[12] a top performer in several fields: stand-up comedy, writing, and film directing. As he tells his story in *Born Standing Up,* he committed himself to doing "consistent work" on his material, making small adjustments to become ever better. Once, at a show delivered in a Vanderbilt University classroom, he finished his act, but no one in the audience of 100 students left. He started picking up his props and still the students remained sitting. Finally, he said, "It's over."

No movement.

He realized the only way out of the room was through the audience, so he headed for the door, walking among the crowd and ad-libbing. The delighted audience followed him out the door and into the campus, where the merry revelers and its surprised leader came upon an empty swimming pool. "Everybody into the pool!" Martin yelled, and then he "swam" across a sea of upstretched arms. Reflecting later on the evening, Martin realized he had "entered new comic territory."

Top performers improve in just this way, experimenting in small ways as they deliver results. Each small improvement makes them better. They focus on learning specific things and avoid self-defeating lofty greatness-type goals. As Martin puts it: "I learned a lesson: It was easy to be great. Every entertainer has a night when everything is clicking. These nights are accidental and statistical: like lucky cards in poker, you can count on them occurring over time. What was hard was to be good, consistently good, night after night, no matter what the abominable circumstances." Top performers work on being good, and leave the judgments about greatness to others: the audience, the critics, customers, and bosses.

Great teams do the same thing. They work on making small improvements, one step at a time. Consider the story told by Mark McClusky about the team of British cyclers[13] who dominated the global field of competitors. In *Faster, Higher, Stronger: How Sports Science Is Creating a New Generation of Superathletes—and What We Can Learn from Them,* McClusky relates how coach Dave Brailsford's team achieved greatness not through "luck or plucky can-do spirit." They did it through the "aggregation of marginal gains." McClusky explains: "Instead of looking for one earth-shattering change, British cycling takes a different approach. It looks at every aspect of performance, and tries to improve each a little bit—even just a tenth of a percent." Steve Martin improved the same way, paying attention every night to the small changes he made—modifying just a tenth of a percent—and steadily enhanced his routine.

To work on small-step changes with your team, start by using "*feedforward*". Why feedforward? Tradi-

Feedforward Tips
Focus on the future, not the past
Pair one critique with two suggestions for the future
Be concrete
Highlight the positive impact the changes will have

tional feedback is important, but it tends to be heavily focused on what went wrong in the past rather than what can be done differently in the future. Leadership coach Marshall Goldsmith coined this term[14] to highlight the importance of getting team members to look ahead toward specific ways to make positive change. To see how this works, consider a colleague who always shows up late to meetings. Rather than telling him, "You're always late and it prevents us from getting to important items on our agenda," imagine saying something along the lines of: "If you aim to be at meetings ten minutes early, it will help us make sure we can get started on time and hit every item on our agenda."

This feedforward empowers your colleagues by helping them think about proactive steps they can make to improve in the future rather than focusing on past failures. It shows the potential positive effects of a change. Rather than dwelling on what has gone wrong, it reduces defensiveness by focusing on what can be done differently. Practice feedforward with your team by creating a rule that any criticisms about past behavior need to be paired with one or two suggestions about what can be done in the future to create a positive change. You can set the tone by asking for feedforward about your own role on the team.

3. Alter the Environment

It is not easy being a jet-lagged American walking the streets of London. New World residents have a dangerous tendency to blunder into traffic coming from an unaccustomed direction—the right. Public authorities came up with a brilliantly simple solution to this problem. They painted two words on the street at the entrance to the crosswalk: "Look right!" Thankfully, this little reminder has saved many lives, including ours on business trips across the pond.

In addition to being a life-saving reminder, the pedestrian signs of London reveal an important fact about changing behavior: it often requires more than will power. When it comes to acting on a commitment, you might imagine you can "just do it." But research shows that pure will-power is unlikely to be effective if the environment encourages old behaviors. Recall the story of PharmTec's change leader, Jenny, and the challenge she faced when she realized that everything about the company's environment contradicted the new values that were being shouted from the corporate mountaintop. How could she expect her reports to become more patient-centric when even the plaques on the wall encouraged them to help out pharm reps first?

You can alter your team's environment to make it more support-ive of desired behaviors. Simple reminders often make the difference between success and failure. We think of reminders as "nudges."[15] We borrow the term from *Nudge,* Cass Sunstein and Richard Thaler's study of "choice architecture." Nudges promote decisions that support a set of goals or policies. The simple reminders on London street corners are an example. You can use similar ideas to encourage the take-up of new behaviors on your team.

One of the most effective nudges you can use is a checklist. Checklists help HPTs in cockpits, oil tankers, and hospitals perform the right tasks, in the right way, at the right time. Consider, for example, the massive problem of containing a virus like Ebola. What separates contagion and containment comes down to little details, like using three pairs of gloves instead of one, and applying hand sanitizer after stripping off each layer. It might seem easy to follow basic procedures for removing parts of a protective suit in a particular order. But remember that doctors treating Ebola patients are often physically and mentally exhausted by the end of a shift; under these circumstances, following the most rudimentary sequence of steps can be a challenge. When experienced professionals are tired and stressed, mistakes happen.

The most basic behaviors are easy to overlook, but they make all the difference in achieving success. As Atul Gawande observes,[16] the operating room checklist for surgeons begins with a deceptively simple question: Am I operating on the correct patient? Perhaps an obvious question, but one that is easy to forget for that very reason. In the case of Ebola, the Centers for Disease Control and Prevention (CDC) created a tailored checklist—a set of procedures that would instill new habits in care providers that are appropriate for managing the unique characteristics of this virus. The Ebola situation demonstrates how powerful checklists can be for reminding your team of the behaviors they need to follow.

Another powerful type of reminder is what we like to call an "accountability buddy." This is our version of a gym buddy, who helps you meet your fitness goals. If you are trying to set better deadlines, or be more transparent about your opinions, ask a team member to observe your behavior and remind you when you are falling back into old patterns. Ask them to coach you on following through on your commitment. Accountability buddies are powerful because they leverage the power of positive social pressure.

Social pressure may be more valuable than money. Consider the conclusions reached by a team of Harvard and Yale[17] social scientists who wanted to know why some groups achieve important collective goals and others fall short. The researchers studied different attempts to induce California residents to decrease water consumption during a recent drought. They found that the simple act of distributing mailers comparing water use among neighbors had the same effect as imposing a 10 percent price increase on water consumption. People who learned about the successful efforts others were making felt motivated to take action, too. The mailer leveraged social pressure to create positive change. Accountability buddies can help your team do the same.

In short, altering your team's environment by creating simple nudges makes behavioral change an easy choice, not an uphill battle.

4. Become Realistic Optimists

Leadership guru Jim Collins[18] has shown that successful leaders are "productively paranoid." HPTs have a similar collective mindset, which psychologist Albert Bandura calls "realistic optimism."[19]

Everybody knows about the power of positive thinking. What many people believe about it, however, can be surprisingly wrong. Sure, it is pleasurable to think positive thoughts and imagine success—picture your team stepping to the stage at the annual corporate meeting to receive the award for excellence. But this fantasy can make you feel *too good*. When you feel good, you relax and run the risk of underperforming.

An HPT goes out of its way to anticipate problems. HPTs from top military units to cyber security groups use so-called Red Teams to reveal all of the risks inherent in a given strategic direction. Red Teams are either groups of insiders or knowledgeable outsiders who test a strategy by trying their best to defeat it. An elite hacker group might try to use whatever tools they can to infiltrate their company's IT security infrastructure, probing to find any weaknesses that may not have been thought of. Red Teams reduce groupthink and make sure your team's change strategy prepares for challenges that might arise.

Your own version of a Red Team could be someone in your group who is assigned the role of devil's advocate in your meetings, or it could be an external party you consult. The point is to make sure your thinking stays grounded in reality and accounts for the inevitable barriers that could lead to failure.

Go ahead and imagine how good it will feel to have worked out tomorrow. But follow up that exercise by dwelling on how miserable you will feel when the alarm goes off at 5 A.M. Then walk yourself through the steps you will take to actually get out of bed, put on your workout clothes, and head off to the gym before sunrise. For example: "*If* I wake up feeling exhausted and just want to pull the covers over my head, *then* I will turn to my right, switch on the lamp, and let the momentum of my movements carry my legs over the side of the bed and onto the floor." Tomorrow morning at 5 A.M.—*voilà*—you are standing up ready to get dressed! No magic here—just the effects of implementing the fourth step of the STAR process.

Best-selling author Caroline Arnold[20] has a term for small commitments like turning on the bedside lamp when the alarm sounds: microresolutions. A simple microresolution that HPTs nearly always make is to debrief a decision after it is made. Over time, the team develops the habit of reflection. The concept of reflection by itself is abstract. But note that the simple act of reflecting on outcomes turns an abstraction into an observable and measurable behavior. You can *observe* the action and *count* the number of times you perform it. Link reflecting with anticipating barriers, and you have a powerful combination.

You should also move from reflection to action in testing the feasibility of your planned changes. The concept of running small experiments originates in the popular *Lean Startup* approach to product development,[21] but the principle behind the concept also applies to HPTs. Commit to finding small ways to test whether actions you want to take will work for your team and how they might be adjusted to overcome any problems you might encounter. Aiming for small adjustments and iterating rapidly, rather than taking on large-scale transformational changes all at once, is the key to successful behavior modifications and to maintaining momentum.

The Enormous Flywheel

Writing in the early twentieth century, the American psychologist William James[22] called habit the "enormous flywheel of society." It is easy to see why. Habits form the basis of the cultural rules that hold together teams, organizations, and societies. Cultivating habits by acting like a STAR is also the means through which individuals and groups enhance their performance in sports, art, science, business, and indeed any activity that drives toward a goal.

One of our clients acted like a STAR in turning around the behavior of a teammate who was underperforming in the most dramatic and disturbing way. Soon after Paul Smithey took over his state's multibillion-dollar Medicaid unit, he heard from several people about an employee—call him Mark—who was simply not working, doing literally nothing all day except pushing paper around. One day, Paul stopped by Mark's cubicle to have a conversation and noticed huge stacks of documents piled everywhere. Afterward, Mark's officemates approached Paul and cryptically urged him to "check the closet." After hours, when Paul opened the closet door near Mark's cubicle, he made a horrifying discovery.

Mark had been moving documents from his desk and depositing them in the closet without even reading them. Paul was stunned. Responsible for following up on drunk driving citations, Mark had allowed hundreds of dangerous drivers to continue traveling the roads. Many bosses would have given Mark a high-minded lecture about the ethics of doing one's job and then fired him—with good reason. Instead, Paul invited the mother of a young man recently killed by a drunk driver to talk with Mark about the importance of his work and how much it meant to her. Her story brought him to tears, and he became one of the most engaged and productive members of Paul's team. The encounter with the grieving mother was the specific nudge—and the inspiration—Mark needed to start doing his work, do it passionately, and continue doing it every day. This nudge also set off positive ripple effects across the whole organization, sending a powerful message that dramatic change was possible.

Inspired by Aristotle, American philosopher Will Durant famously observed, "We are what we repeatedly do. Excellence, then, is not an act, but a habit."[23] In the same way, HPTs are what they repeatedly do. They are thus always working hard to close the saying-doing gap. In setting commitments, they begin a process that leads to a meticulous focus on small, repeatable actions that produce a culture of success.

In closing this chapter, let's examine, from beginning to end, how one leader acted like a STAR in using the 3x3 Framework to turn around an underperforming team at major hospital.

Bringing It All Together: The Surgery Team Turnaround

One of our colleagues—call him Vince Taylor—showed what the 3x3 principles can do when he turned around a troubled team at an academic teaching hospital in the Northeastern U.S. After leaving his position at an Ivy League medical center, Taylor took charge of the research team in the hospital's esteemed specialty surgery department. He found what any outsider would call a toxic culture. The team was charged with administrating studies done by more than 10 surgeons in the department—recruiting subjects, obtaining the proper permissions, and tracking results. Cutting-edge research is the lifeblood of any academic medicine department, but this team had become a clogged artery.

Team members sometimes spent more time gossiping about each other than working on their assigned projects. The surgeons who relied on them complained bitterly about the low productivity of the team and the high turnover of leadership and staff. It didn't help matters that the department was juggling over 100 projects, some of them complex and high-risk. Taylor had been tasked with nothing less than reforming the division.

His first step was to **establish new commitments**. The team's counterproductive behaviors had been driven by a culture in which the most prominent unwritten rule was: "If you make a mistake, you will be an outcast." In the first meeting with his new team, Taylor signaled a new direction when he introduced his key leadership principle: "If you struggle, we will give you the resources to succeed." This became a kind of mantra. He made it clear that mistakes would be approached as a learning opportunity. Staff would be supported to maximize opportunities for success rather than castigated to minimize the chances of failure. He repeated his mantra in every meeting.

Taylor also knew that changing the culture would be more than a simple matter of issuing a grand proclamation. Transformation takes persistence and attention to detail, and the old culture was likely to continue living on in the everyday habits of his staff. Ever the careful observer, Taylor made note of team behaviors to **check the alignment** between the new values his team had committed to and what they actually did in the office. He knew it would take hard work to achieve that alignment.

Sure enough, he began hearing complaints about a young assistant, Katie, who was struggling to keep up with her duties. Before Taylor arrived, Katie was a terribly disorganized project manager. Her former supervisor had perversely lowered expectations as her performance flagged. For example, Katie was so frequently late to work that her official start time was changed from 8:30 A.M. to 9 A.M. The upshot: she started showing up at 9:10 A.M.

Co-workers began pushing for Katie to be fired. They called her a "lost cause" and an "underachiever." But Taylor, who had been trained in anthropological methods, saw Katie's difficulties as a product of the old departmental culture rather than a sign of personal failings.

Instead of punishing Katie and perpetuating a destructive cycle, Taylor aimed to *close the saying-doing gap.* He supported Katie as he had committed to do. Looking back, it might seem obvious that he did the right thing. But remember the amount of pressure he was under at the time. He was a new director taking over a team supporting surgeons, most of whom expected quick results. When Taylor was confronted with a young, inexperienced employee who was clearly underperforming and whom most of the team wanted out, the obvious thing was not so obvious. It would have been much easier for him to appease the team by firing Katie and relieving himself of a substantial burden in the process. Putting his commitment into action in a stressful situation was by no means easy. What it required was a process and a focus on manageable change.

To be effective, Taylor focused on behaviors. He translated his mantra into concrete actions and helped Katie by focusing on behaviors she could change. The goal was to establish new, positive habits. Rather than setting low expectations and hoping Katie would meet them, Taylor set the bar higher and challenged Katie to surpass them.

Taylor began with a simple habit—showing up on time. He sat the young manager down and said, "From now on, you're going to get here at 8 A.M." Katie was perplexed. If she had had trouble getting to the office at 8:30 A.M., how would it help to set the start time even earlier? Taylor told her that they would arrive together, giving her the nudge and support she needed to change her bad habit. Katie began setting her alarm earlier and was never late again.

Much to the team's surprise, Taylor began giving Katie more responsibility, not less. The team nearly had a panic attack when Taylor put Katie in charge of supporting an external audit on their compliance practices. Even the doctors Taylor's team supported were worried because of the visibility of the audit—any errors could delay important research.

It was a risky move, but it paid off. Katie discovered a talent for interpersonal relationships that she leveraged to keep the auditors happy and calm the anxieties of the surgeons about the process. Her performance improved so quickly, she ended up being promoted twice in short succession. The key to Katie's success was the way Taylor was able to change how she thought about her work. She had seen herself as a useless paper pusher, and the team culture reinforced that perception. Taylor showed her how her administrative responsibilities were the rock supporting the team, and he used specific tools and nudges to change Katie's behavior accordingly.

HPT Takeaways

Think Like a STAR

To close the saying-doing gap, avoid abstract discussions and focus on concrete behavioral changes.

Be Specific

Target changes that matter most and emphasize observable actions.

Take Small Steps

Transformational change starts with small adjustments. Begin by asking what small steps your team members can make toward aligning with their commitments.

Alter the Environment

Change is usually not a product of willpower alone. Ask: What can you alter about the work context to nudge your team toward the right behaviors?

Be a Realistic Optimist

Make a plan for dealing with the inevitable setbacks that will arise.

The hard work Taylor put into this reflective process with Katie and other members of the team paid dividends. Morale shot through the roof during his tenure, and the surgeons who complained previously about the group's work praised the surge in productivity they saw. He helped bring in many new research projects and transformed a money-losing division into a surplus-generating operation. The word spread around the university about the good work environment. People would stop in to ask if there were job openings and several people were hired.

Taylor's experience shows that creating and maintaining an HPT does not necessarily require heroic efforts or a soaring vision. It involves a continuous process of observation, reflection and adjustment focused on the small behaviors that lead to big differences in performance. Team leaders need not move mountains. It is more effective to close small gaps that make the difference between a team-in-name and a true HPT.

4 Pay Attention: The Seven Common Mistakes You Are Probably Making

An elite member of the U.S. Army's Special Forces, the soldier approaches the Vietcong camp alone. His mission is limited: locate a group of POWs. But after learning the enemy soldiers are being supported and trained by the Soviet army, he decides to single-handedly free the American captives. Not even a platoon of fighters is enough to stop the highly trained commando. After hijacking a helicopter, he lands in the middle of the POW base and destroys the enemy force before flying the prisoners to safety.

If this scene sounds vaguely familiar, it may be because you have seen it in the movie *Rambo: First Blood Part II*. Even if you have not watched this Sylvester Stallone classic, it probably sounds similar to the plot of numerous other action movies featuring the lone hero soldier. This figure is always a courageous warrior who has risen through the ranks of the most elite military and security units in the world, such as the Secret Service, Army Rangers, or Navy SEALs. He has been prepared by a hellish training regimen to march into enemy

territory and subdue large forces with his first-rate combat skills and
killer instincts.

Wowed by an endless procession of Hollywood blockbusters (we
admit to being fans ourselves), many people have come to think of elite
military teams as being collections of well-trained individuals, able to
accomplish dangerous feats through sheer force and grit. But take a
moment to compare the scene from *First Blood* to the description of an
actual raid conducted during the fight against Al Qaeda in Iraq.

Real-World Teamwork

A SEAL team has just raided an Al Qaeda safe house in an overnight
mission in search of a high-level operative. Afterward, as the soldiers
catch some much-needed sleep, a young intelligence analyst is monitoring drone footage of the site when she notices a strange vehicle
pull up and then quickly drive away. She immediately calls another
group of soldiers who spring into action. Moments later, they are at the
controls of two helicopters and tracking the vehicle through a maze of
streets. The intelligence team back at the American base analyzes likely
routes the vehicle will take and sends the information to the airborne
SEAL teams in real time.

All of a sudden, the vehicle stops and exchanges a passenger with
a second one that speeds off in a different direction. The SEAL team
blocks the first one as intelligence analysts track the second. The
team quickly discovers that the original vehicle is now being driven by
low-level fighters and realize that their target is elsewhere. The SEALs
adjust immediately, working with the intelligence team to locate and
blockade the second vehicle, which is carrying the Al Qaeda operative.
Less than an hour after fleeing the safe house, he is in custody.

Former general Stan McChrystal, in his book *Team of Teams*,[1]
gave the account of this actual raid. It is clearly very different from the
scenarios depicted in countless action movies. Instead of a single heroic
fighter taking on a whole army, a network of soldiers and analysts in
different locations work together seamlessly, adjusting in real time to
capture a single high-level target.

Intense give-and-take drives teamwork success in today's military. But not just there: in a global marketplace characterized by dense connectivity, where small shifts in one industry can create large-scale, unpredictable competitive transformations elsewhere, high-performing teamwork is a must-have. HPTs perform and learn at the same time, adjusting as circumstances change, like the SEAL team in Iraq.

A Lesson in High-Performing Teamwork

McChrystal arrived in post-Hussein Iraq thinking he would be able to stop the Al Qaeda threat with the same, top-down, "command and control"–style leadership that had characterized conventional military operations. He and his colleagues quickly found their approach was largely useless against a different type of enemy. Highly decentralized and able to strike quickly, this enemy had no need for the skills and training of a conventional army. McChrystal's team had to adjust on the fly by creating a more networked fighting force characterized by high levels of trust, autonomy, and transparency. In the process, they revolutionized twenty-first century combat.

The mistakes made by McChrystal's team in becoming an HPT were the same ones we see all the time in organizations around the world. Misaligned priorities, poor information-sharing, unseen situational factors, confused roles—these are common failings that hinder teams from achieving their full potential, and they can crop up in each step of the 3x3 process. Watching for these mistakes is the first step to overcoming them.

So let's make a list of mistakes—and check it, and keep checking it. Remember: teamwork is a continual process of aligning and realigning. Mistakes will happen.

The Seven Common Mistakes You Are Probably Making

Our philosophy is that teams have great potential but it is hard to realize it. In the same way, our 3x3 Framework has been proven to deliver results, but you have to work hard to apply it. Implementing the three steps takes discipline and high levels of situational awareness. It is all too easy to get off track.

Our research and experience tells us that all aspects of the 3x3 Framework are associated with typical mistakes. In this final chapter of Part One, we illustrate each one. Get in the habit of watching for these mistakes. Your team is probably making one or more of them.

Trust us—we continue to make these same mistakes ourselves. Remember: HPTs are not perfect, but they are committed to getting better, step by step.

Seven Mistakes

1. Overemphasizing Abstract Goals

Contrary to popular belief, in the real world of elite fighting units, soldiers with a Rambo mentality usually fail to make it through the first week of training. Take the Navy SEALs basic training course, BUD/S—a six-month regimen of navigating obstacle courses, running underwater missions, and learning sophisticated combat techniques, all punctuated with punishments like "surf torture" (lying on a beach, with chilly waves washing over you) for those who fail a test. This may sound like the perfect program for crafting a Stallone-like hero dedicated to abstract values like "Freedom" and "Justice." But according to Coleman Ruiz, officer in charge[2] of one of the BUD/S phases, it is exactly these types of recruits who get weeded out. They are focused on the wrong goals.

Avoid Abstract Goals

Ruiz can tell right away in early interviews just who is unlikely to finish: those wannabes who talk vaguely about wanting to "take on the challenge" of training. Actually, the defining aspect of training is not the physical challenge, it is the specific commitment to support your teammates.

Of course, the BUD/S program isn't exactly a light jog on the treadmill. You regularly run four miles on wet sand in boots. You plow through tough ropes courses. You take off and exchange diving gear underwater without coming up for a breath. We humbly submit that we would probably wind up in "surf torture" more than a few times. But the point is that, while a very select few are able to become SEALs, many hundreds of thousands of athletic Americans who run marathons, cross-train, or swim regularly could likely meet the fitness criteria.

The difference between an elite SEAL and a weekend warrior is in the personal priorities that the training is designed to drag into the light of day. The dropouts generally fail not because they can't do the training—they simply realize they don't want to. As Ruiz recounts to McChrystal, "They just had different priorities. . . .[W]e had a saying that they would leave because of 'my girlfriend, my dog, my cat, and my checkbook.' They can take it, they just realize it isn't for them."

The BUD/S training is a reminder that transcendent goals are not enough to get the most out of your teammates. Such goals are important, to be sure. JFK would not have been able to inspire NASA and an entire country to support the lunar mission without the powerful vision of making a round trip to the surface of the moon. But remember that it was also important for him to align powerful political factions, each of which was motivated by narrow WIIFM considerations.

People like to talk about transcendent goals for a good reason. Such goals are uplifting, and they make work meaningful and feel less like drudgery. But when teams overestimate the importance of inspiring vision during the goal-setting stage, they risk paying too little attention to aligning personal priorities and relationships with the big goals. Are our team members truly committed to each other? Or are they worried that their work will detract from other projects and obligations they have elsewhere in the organization or at home?

HPTs make sure that big, collective goals align with small, personal commitments that drive performance.

2. Underemphasizing Roles

On June 16, 2015, NBA player Andre Iguodala stood on a podium in the QuickenLoans[3] Arena, accepting the Finals MVP trophy for his role in helping the Golden State Warriors defeat the Cleveland Cavaliers. Many sportswriters saw Iguodala as the underdog. He beat out arguably the best player in the world—namely, LeBron James—as well as the regular season MVP from the Warriors, Stephen Curry. Still, no one was surprised that Iguodala, a former all-star, was capable of playing at such a high level. What shocked fans was that he spent a good part of the regular season on the bench.

Iguodala's success had everything to do with the way rookie coach Steve Kerr had managed the Warriors all season. Kerr's philosophy is captured in the team-first motto, "Strength in Numbers," that the players took to heart. Contrast the Warriors' success with another basketball team's surprising failure. The 2004 U.S. Olympic squad comprised some of the world's best talent, bringing together future hall-of-famers like Allen Iverson, Tim Duncan, and a young LeBron James. They were supposed to march undefeated on their way to the gold, as the previous three Olympic teams had done, but the all-stars were upset by less-talented teams multiple times and struggled to win a bronze medal.

Clear Up Role Confusion

The accepted story is one about star players with "attitude problems" who were in it for themselves. But actually the team played with playoff-level intensity, making the defeats all the more disappointing and puzzling. Like the Olympic team members, Iguodala himself was a proud star—he once joked that he would kill coach Kerr for benching him if the team didn't win the championship. Why did the Warriors succeed when a team with more individual talent lost to lesser competitors?

The problem was in the Olympic squad's structure. The team was loaded with talented players who were skilled at driving toward the basket, but it lacked long-distance shooters. As a result, it was difficult for the team to open up defenses. Manu Ginobli, a player on the Argentinean team[4] that won the gold, would later observe: "I saw their roster and I knew we would beat them." Many of the American players joined the team just two months before the Olympics, just after the NBA season had ended. The coaches had little time to find the proper role for each player. Their challenge mirrors the issue many teams have with creating roles: they simply fail to do it.

Teams often make the mistake of assuming they can just focus on assembling the best talent and worry about roles later. There is some truth in this assumption—in Chapter 6 you will learn about startup teams that have operated successfully in this way. But the key is that after learning about the raw talent on a team, a good leader will eventually create roles that capitalize on strengths. Short on time, the Olympic coaches were unable to take this step.

Kerr had both the time and the coaching skill to get the most out of his players by putting them in the right positions. Most coaches would never bench a franchise player like Iguodala. And not only was he benched—Iguodala was backing up Harrison Barnes, a third-year forward whose poor performance in the previous season had earned him boos from hometown fans. Iguodala himself was apprehensive about the move when the new coach approached him about it in preseason. But he agreed to go along with the idea because Kerr was able to articulate a compelling explanation for how all the pieces fit together to make a championship contender.

Kerr had a clear understanding of roles. He believed Barnes had struggled after a promising rookie season because his confidence was hurt when he was moved to a reserve role in his second year. Barnes needed the security of having a consistent role on the team, and he would improve by being forced to keep up with better players. Iguodala would provide a solid veteran presence for the bench unit and a boost of energy later in games when starters rested. As it happened, both players excelled in their roles. Barnes returned to form while Iguodala became a serious candidate for the Sixth Man of the Year award, and they helped the Warriors win their first title in 40 years. While no one would question that Iguodala was a better player than Barnes, it made sense for the team to have Barnes in the starting role.

The contrast between the two teams shows that brains and brawn are not the most important team characteristics. Well-structured teams generally outperform those with more raw talent—strength, skill, or IQ.

3. Undervaluing Relationships

One of the most common mistakes in creating norms is to neglect relationship building. It may seem like superficial "soft" stuff. But actually it is the superconductor that keeps teams in sync and makes them adaptable. Adaptability often adds up to dollars and cents. It can also save lives.

Don't Ignore
Relationships

Consider another example from McChrystal's experience in Iraq. McChrystal came into a situation in which analysts were loath to share crucial intelligence with each other for fear that it would diminish their role or that another agency would misinterpret the data. Days would often pass after a raid on an enemy target before information in confiscated computers and notebooks was analyzed and sent back to headquarters. By that time, terrorist cells would have dispersed and attack plans would have been altered. The value of the intelligence had spoiled like fruit left out on the counter.

One of McChrystal's solutions: Embed key personnel with different agencies on six-month rotations. He called them linchpin liaison officers (LNOs). The LNOs would develop relationships within their host organization and report back regularly to their superiors about their vantage point of the conflict. Great idea in theory, but in practice the LNOs quickly ran into the same silos they were sent to break down. One SEAL placed with a U.S. embassy in a Middle-Eastern country found himself cold-shouldered by his new colleagues, who virtually ignored him when he first arrived. With nothing better to do, he began emptying out trash around the facility to make himself useful.

Seeing that he would have to do more to build trust, McChrystal took a risk with new norms of collaboration. He sent some of his best people on these assignments, and he regularly fed them high quality intelligence to pass on to their host. His gamble paid off. Instead of taking advantage of McChrystal's team norms and hoarding credit for important information, agencies began responding in kind. McChrystal noticed the shift when they started sharing some of their very best people with him. Information flowed more freely, and each stakeholder in the battle against Al Qaeda gained a broad, unified sense of the ebb and flow of the conflict. McChrystal calls this "collective consciousness."

Because relationship building is inefficient, teams so often neglect to create norms for it. No doubt, it takes time and energy. But it pays dividends in situations characterized by uncertainty and change, when flexibility is your most important asset.

A recent study on leadership styles reached this conclusion in a simulated environment not unlike the one that McChrystal's task force faced. Researchers from three universities formed teams[5] of random participants to compete in a computer-based battle simulation in which each individual had different roles and levels of access to information. To succeed, the teams had to collaborate efficiently, just like any corporate team in a dynamic market. The teams were divided into two types: those run in a top-down fashion by highly directive leaders, and those that were more decentralized, where individuals had autonomy to make decisions and collaborate with others as they saw fit. What they found confirms McChrystal's experience.

The teams that emphasized trust-building and autonomy got off to a much slower start without the efficiency of blindly following orders dictated quickly by a single leader. However, as the simulation went on, the empowered teams consistently outperformed the "command and control" style teams. The relationships they had built internally enabled them to quickly share information. They also knew who should work together on a particular task. As the environment changed, complexity hampered the directive leaders, who became a bottleneck for their teams. The decentralized groups were able to adapt and adjust on the fly.

Building relationships is not quick or easy. But this does not mean you should fall into the common trap of dismissing relationship-building when creating team norms. It may seem like the "soft stuff," but the payoffs are clear: flexibility, adaptability, and high performance.

4. Making Too Many Rules

We have emphasized the importance of creating the rules that shape your team's culture and drive performance. But the biggest mistake teams make overall in this first step is to try to make rules for every possible situation. This starts with an understandable impulse: you want to plan for all contingencies. The problem is that reality is just too complex.

Simplify the Rules

Caroline Lim, the top HR executive at the world's largest port company,[6] says she learned about the significance of culture during her time as a senior leader at Apple. Seeing how in sync everyone seemed to be whether or not the boss was around, she realized "culture is about what people do when no one is watching." We agree—and we would add that you often express culture without even realizing it. There are simply too many unspoken rules that you follow moment to moment to account for every single one of them.

The solution is to focus on making the rules that matter as you establish commitments—the simple, keystone habits that will lead to deep cultural change across a range of behaviors, like a chain reaction.

Starbucks founder Howard Schultz[7] knows how to focus on rules that matter. Schultz returned to the company as CEO in 2008, when shareholders and the media alike were saying the retailer had lost its touch. Sales were declining. There were plans to shutter 100 U.S. stores. The stock price had dropped 54 percent over the previous two years. Fast food chains were cutting into Starbucks's market share with cheaper coffee. In perhaps the greatest blow to Schultz's sense of pride, McDonald's brew had beaten Starbucks in the Consumer Reports rankings the previous year.

Schultz replaced CEO Jim McDonald with a promise to bring the ailing company "back to the future." What had gone wrong? Schultz believed that the company's success had made its leaders feel compelled to do too much. In a brutally honest internal memo, Schultz blamed the company's tarnished brand on the fact that they had been so focused on multiple goals related to relentless growth, efficiency, and the customer experience that they had failed to excel in any one area in particular.

His solution? Bring back the practice of grinding beans in-store. He rolled out a plan to have bean-grinders running every time a fresh batch of drip coffee was made. In switching to pre-ground coffee, Starbucks had increased the speed of customer flow at the expense of the "romance and theater" of buying a cup of great coffee. Schultz wrote: "We achieved fresh-roasted bagged coffee, but at what cost? The loss of aroma—perhaps the most powerful nonverbal signal we had in our stores." Rather than trying to do everything, Schultz's plan was to get back to basics by focusing on the coffee house experience that had been the foundation of Starbucks's success. He started with a simple rule: have baristas grind the beans.

On your own team, it can be tempting to try to fix everything at once. But you may end up with a long list of rules that is impossible to implement. Focus instead on the few rules that are likely to have the biggest impact on your team's culture and performance. Avoid trying to do everything. Just "grind the beans."

5. Ignoring Reflection

When your team seems to have reached agreement on "the way we do things around here," you might feel like kicking back and enjoying your hard-won accomplishment.

Make Time for Reflection

We have bad news for you: your hard-won accomplishment is fleeting.

Because the four horsemen of unpredictable change—volatility, uncertainty, complexity, and ambiguity, or VUCA[8]—are always at your heels, you have to stay focused on the 3x3 Framework. The strong culture a team creates to solve one set of problems can become a barrier for solving new problems that arise in a VUCA world. Focused on getting work done, teams often make the mistake of going through the second step of the 3x3 too infrequently. Many teams have one big reflection session at an annual retreat. But it is better to have more frequent, shorter check-ins. When teams give short shrift to checking assumptions, they drift out of alignment with each other and the external environment.

Such was the case of SEAL Team 6. Earlier we described how SEAL teams are disciplined and unselfish. But this was not always true of the most elite and legendary SEAL team of all—one that has been the subject of movies, books, and video games. Team 6 was born out of a failed rescue attempt during the 1980 Iranian hostage crisis. In response, SEAL commander Dick Marcinko[9] was charged with creating an elite counterterrorism unit to complement the Army's Delta Force. Marcinko believed the Delta Force had developed a culture that was obsessed with procedures and discipline. He aimed to create a team that was leaner and more "out of the box" to take on the toughest missions.

Marcinko was certainly the man to form such a squad. Feared and revered for his reputation as a loose cannon, Marcinko shaped a renegade culture that quickly took root among his elite recruits. Team 6 operatives became known for their reckless behavior. They routinely crashed cars in training exercises. Their idea of team bonding was mixing it up in drunken bar brawls. This promoted "unit frigging integrity," Marcinko explained, only he used a stronger word that he was known for dropping multiple times in every sentence.

Marcinko saw the strong culture as an asset at the time of Team 6's formation. He argued that only a highly creative squad could pursue seemingly impossible missions as it operated covertly in dark, seedy corners of the world. Marcinko ruffled feathers, but he seemed to get results. Team 6 has executed some of the most legendary missions in military history, including the killing of Osama Bin Laden and the rescue of Captain Phillips.

However, this culture had a downside. It isolated Team 6 from the rest of the military establishment. After a while, no one asked whether the Team 6 modus operandi needed to be adjusted or improved in any way. The lack of oversight went to extremes. Congressman and former Team 6 officer Ryan Zinke recounts[10] in a *New York Times* interview how, during preparations for the 1992 Olympics, he escorted an admiral to a bar where the group was relaxing after exercises: "When we opened the door, it reminded me of *Pirates of the Caribbean*," Mr. Zinke said, recalling that the admiral was appalled by the operators' long hair, beards, and earrings. 'My Navy?' the admiral asked him. 'These guys are in my Navy?'"

The team's successes had dissuaded Navy leadership from checking on which parts of the strong Team 6 culture worked, and which could cause problems. The inattention led to several widely reported incidents. One occurred in the Afghanistan conflict: a lieutenant commander led his team on a wild joyride through the countryside, blowing through checkpoints until gunfire from local militiamen forced them to surrender. The individualistic Team 6 culture also showed its dark side when former members leaked sensitive details of operations to secure book and video game contracts.

The Navy has since worked to recalibrate the Team 6 culture. The distinctive Team 6 edginess is now balanced with a commitment to the Navy's professional values and mission. On your own team, remember that check-ins need not always be huge affairs reserved for day-long company retreats. They can be as simple as a weekly stand-up meeting.

6. Failing to Sell the Change

When Mickey Drexler was hired for the top spot at J. Crew[11] in 2003, he was expected to engineer a turnaround for the ailing retailer just as he had for Gap Inc. in the 1990s. Drexler earned the moniker "Merchant Prince" for paring down the Gap clothing line to minimalist khakis and button-down basics. In the process, he launched a "casual chic" fashion movement that inspired a whole generation of young shoppers. At the Gap, Drexler was known for his kinetic,

Bring Others Along

hyperactive energy. He was frequently heard yelling from his office and sent his colleagues countless voicemails that talked up half-baked ideas. As Gap grew into a corporate behemoth, several board members began to feel the company required a leader who was less of a freewheeling spirit. Eventually, after a few well-documented missteps, Drexler left.

But J. Crew enthusiastically welcomed Drexler's energy. It was the corrective needed for the drab, suburban look that characterized the company's offerings. Drexler joined J. Crew less than a year after being let go from the Gap. Turnaround 2 was, at first, equally dramatic. He focused the brand on quality apparel for young people who had graduated from the Gap and were willing to pay a little more for style. When the Obama family was seen wearing J. Crew on talk shows and at the president's inauguration, Drexler felt the brand had come into its own.

Drexler then seemed to lose his touch again. Revenue dropped significantly. The market downturn of the late 2000s played a part. But there was also a creeping sense among even J. Crew's most loyal shoppers that the brand was suffering an identity crisis. Enthusiasts who had frequently posted pictures of outfits with the hashtag #JCrew-everything began pleading #reviveJCrew. After having successfully taken the company public, Drexler helped cobble together a private equity buyout that many saw as a raw deal for shareholders. But the deal was done. The Merchant Prince had muscled it through.

Still, the company continued to struggle, triggering layoffs amid slumping sales. Shoppers remained confused about whether the company represented upscale fashion or affordable young professional attire. The split-personality brand was obvious in the stores, where you could get a free pastry on National Donut Day and peruse regularly discounted items placed next to a $450 neon ombré sequined sweater.

Drexler made the same mistake as Johnson at JC Penney. He failed to keep his people motivated about the change he wanted to make. His turn-around ended up being a one-man cause rather than a true team effort. Schisms in the J.Crew leadership team about the adjustments the company needed to make led to the confusion in its brand strategy.

For example, powerhouse creative director Jenna Lyons clashed with Drexler frequently on what the brand should represent. She wanted to focus on pricier, trendy fashion where Drexler saw a need to cut price and go basic to compete with the cheaper H&Ms of the world.

One of the most common pitfalls team leaders make in closing the saying-doing gap is failing to get buy-in on the change they seek. Too often, they imagine that strength of will or charisma will be enough. It is true that everybody likes a hero story. But when it comes to committed teamwork, heroes are only part of the story. Great or not, they need to bring people along with them.

7. Putting Procedure before Process

Try an experiment. Search the video "selective attention test" online and follow the instructions. You will see basketball players in white T-shirts and black T-shirts. Your goal is to count the number of passes you see. Go ahead, we'll wait. . . .

Remember the Important Things

Did you count 15 passes? If so, then you got the correct number.

But did you see the gorilla walking through the middle of the scene? More than half of viewers fail to see it. The creators of this test, psychologists Christopher Chabris and Daniel Simons, attribute this result to "inattentional blindness."[12] When you are focused on following a specific instruction or fulfilling a designated task, you overlook what should be obvious.

Inattentional blindness comes into play with real-life occurrences that are much more serious than a guy walking around in a gorilla suit. Chabris and Simons created a study that had participants follow a jogger through a park. Unbeknownst to the subjects, a staged beating was taking place just to the side of the road at a certain point along the jogger's route. The results were similar to the video test—even in broad daylight, nearly half of the participants failed to see the person being beaten. They were too focused on carrying out instructions and missed seeing a serious problem.

This tunnel vision is common on teams that become too focused on procedure. This is a common mistake that can crop up anywhere in the 3x3 process. Teams that focus on procedure go through the rote acts of talking about goals, roles, and norms, but the conversations tend to be superficial. Treating chartering, reflecting, and adjusting as primarily box-checking activities can blind your team to the real issues those surface-level procedures are supposed to uncover. Like a jogger unknowingly running past a roadside robbery, you may be focused on flip-charting norms while half of your teammates are uncomfortable speaking up. Remember that the steps we lay out here are a process. The point is to help you make the right observations and have the tough conversations.

The Little Things, and the Big Picture

The seven common mistakes all relate to the biggest issue on teams: ignoring small data. Small data is all about understanding your group's spoken and unspoken priorities and assumptions, gathering insights about your team's dynamics, and taking concrete steps to get beliefs, relationships, and behaviors in alignment. This stands in contrast to the recent big data craze, which is all about gathering a large amount of data about average individuals to predict what they will be like as a group.

In fact, when the idea was first introduced, the hype about big data was that it would make theories obsolete. You would just know everything you needed to know from large datasets. We are fans of large-scale statistics, but we are glad the lofty talk has come back down to Earth. Big data is an important and useful tool, but it does not give you a full portrait of your team. It is not just an aggregation of individuals. It takes on emergent characteristics, behaviors, and shared identities that are different from the sum of its parts.

The 3x3 Framework is all about understanding the little misalignments in your team that can lead to big problems, and identifying small changes in the rules that can get your team back on track. Stepping back from the little things to the big picture, let's summarize the framework:

- Culture is made up the spoken and unspoken rules that govern group behavior.
- The rule-making ability is what enables people to collaborate effectively, but is also the cause of misalignments that can kill team passion and sap performance.
- To make the most of your team culture and build a committed team, you have to:
  1. Establish Commitments around the rules that really matter—the Three Foundations of HPTs:
     - Goals that are clear and inspiring
     - Roles that are well-defined and leverage the skills and interests of each team member
     - Norms that help you manage communication, decision-making, and conflict
  2. Check Alignment by building awareness of the gaps that form between the commitments team members made and what they are actually doing.
  3. Close the Saying-Doing Gap by creating actionable behavioral change.

Managing this process is not easy. Culture is complex and hard to pin down. But if you can commit to the 3x3 Framework and keep an eye out for the common team mistakes, you will be on track to becoming one of those relatively rare groups: a truly high-performing team.

Part Two

P art One was about the 3×3 Framework basics that apply to any team. In Part Two, we narrow our focus down to five specific but common team types. Why these five? Based on our experience as consultants and business school faculty, we bet you spend a good chunk of your time collaborating in ways that resemble one or more of them:

- Virtual teams
- Start-ups
- Innovation projects
- Leadership groups
- Committees

Each chapter highlights the typical headaches that plague these types of collaboration and cause all-too-familiar performance problems. We show how key concepts from Part One can help you tailor solutions. We conclude the book with several observations about current workplace trends that make committed teamwork more necessary than ever.

5 Can You Hear Me Now? Making Virtual Teams Work

"Do we have everyone? Wait—Michael, are you there? Do we have Michael? Well, what do others think—should we wait for him to connect? Or can—should—we get started now? Can people hear me? Hello? Can you hear me now?"

In typical fashion, with a string of questions to which no answers were forthcoming, a recent virtual meeting started at Global Brands International (GBI), the retail company we introduced in Chapter 3. We were sitting with three other participants in an office 37 stories above Manhattan. Across the continent, in San Francisco, two people were linked by videoconference with the five of us in NYC. Three callers in unnamed locations were dialed in to a teleconference line.

An executive named Brian was one of the callers. "I made my best effort to make it into the city," Brian groans against a background of ear-splitting distortion. A moment later, he loses cell phone service and disappears from the line.

The rest of the meeting was just as disjointed. The whole experience was an exercise in frustration.

It is hard enough to communicate under the best of conditions. Virtual teams have an even tougher time of it. Opportunities for misalignment abound. In their 2001 study of 70 virtual teams,

Vijay Govindarajan and Anil Gupta found that[1] 82 percent of virtual teams fell short of their goals and 33 percent rated themselves as largely unsuccessful. A 2005 Deloitte study[2] of IT projects outsourced to virtual work groups found that 66 percent failed to satisfy client requirements.

Performance problems notwithstanding, as technology continues to advance, virtual teams are becoming increasingly common. In today's mobile world, teammates are scattered across offices, homes, coworking spaces, airports, and highways. You can communicate from just about anywhere, even if the conditions are often less than ideal. What you lose in nuance you gain in valuable flexibility, right?

Indeed, for individual team members, flexibility has lots of appeal. If you don't have to drive or fly to meet regularly with your team in the office, you can build your schedule around chores, family obligations, and personal time. Human capital researchers Ellen Ernst Kossek and Kelly Hannum,[3] find that the independence employees gain from flexible schedules boosts their morale, productivity, and engagement.

For organizations, virtual teams are appealing for additional reasons. Projects can be staffed with the most talented and best-suited employees and contractors, no matter where they are located. When you go the route of virtual teaming, you not only get to hire the best talent, you get to keep it, too. A study by the National Work/Life Measurement Project found[4] that 80 percent of employees believe flexible hours make them more likely to stay with their current employer.

Find the best people, make them productive, and retain them for the long haul. Sounds like the best of all possible worlds. Well, almost. In a virtual setting, you are likely to have a hard time with two teamwork essentials: trust and communication. Without the frequent opportunities for face-to-face contact that co-location affords, you have to tweak the 3x3 Framework to reduce the misalignments that so frequently occur.

Just about every team—virtual or in person—will need to do some tweaking, since nearly all of the work done today is at least partly virtual.

You may not think you operate in a virtual environment, but we are pretty certain you communicate with your teammates frequently over the phone and by email, share documents and develop ideas through cloud-based software, or have to videoconference from time to time when someone is out of the office. Virtual teaming, then, is a fact of life. Like it or not, you need to grapple with issues related to trust, communication, and alignment that are raised by digital technologies. In this chapter, we offer some guidance about how to do it.

Build Trust Early

Let's return to the GBI meeting. Even though there was frustration around the less-than-ideal conditions, temperaments were calm and the mood was light.

"Let's just continue, and if Michael can, he'll jump in on the call," Julia suggested. "Michael's always ahead of the game—he already emailed his numbers! We can just catch him up later if he can't connect now." Julia's assumption could have gone the other way in that moment. She could have interpreted Michael's absence as a lack of engagement or respect, as often happens when remote co-workers miss meetings. But Michael had demonstrated his track record of reliability by sending his work ahead of the call. His teammates knew him well enough to believe he would stay on schedule despite the apparent technical difficulties that kept him from participating in this call. In short, his teammates *trusted* him.

Trust is one of the keys to success for any team, but for virtual teams trust is the essential glue to bind teammates together across distances and time zones. If people do not trust others to deliver, they waste time on duplicate efforts, time lines are delayed, and creativity and innovation suffer.

Leadership development expert Sean Graber[5] differentiates between two types of trust: cognitive and affective (see Figure 5.1). Cognitive trust is based on your objective analysis of another's past behavior. The second kind of trust, affective trust, is just as important and harder to build in a virtual setting. Affective trust is the implicit *feeling* that you can trust someone. It comes from a relationship built over time. It is hard to *feel* trust when all you know is somebody's voice or email signature.

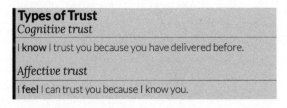

Types of Trust
Cognitive trust
I **know** I trust you because you have delivered before.
Affective trust
I **feel** I can trust you because I know you.

Michael was able to build both types of trust with his teammates because they had collaborated both face-to-face and remotely for years. But you may not have the luxury of so much time, in which case you need to integrate deliberate trusting-building mechanisms into your virtual teaming. Most important, you should make the chartering process as high-contact as you can. If at all possible, even for just the first meeting, bring everyone to the same physical place for setting goals, allocating roles, and establishing norms. This may be expensive, but it can have a huge impact on your team's success. Of course, it is not always possible to have all hands face to face meetings, even when a new team is just getting started. But high-contact communication can include video chats, conference calls, and having at least some teammates meet in the same physical space.

The Egg Principle

"I live south of Belfast in a very rural area."

At a recent BACON Conference, GitHub employee Coby Chapple[6] was telling a story about a simple ritual in his small Irish village. (Not *that* kind of bacon, by the way. He was speaking at a conference for software developers.) He continued: "When I want eggs, I take my dog for about a quarter-mile walk down the road to a red box my neighbor has set up. When you open that box, it's filled with cartons of eggs, with a red lock box to the side. I take a carton of eggs, and leave a pound coin in the lock box, walk home, and cook up some lunch."

"It's awesome," Coby said. "It's convenient, cost-effective, asynchronous. I get to take my dog for an extra walk and help out my neighbor instead of a faceless grocery corporation." But the real value for Coby is even greater: "Most importantly, it makes me feel trusted."

This story, of course, is a metaphor for working remotely. Trust is what makes virtual teams work, and it has to go both ways, as it did and does for Coby. He trusts that eggs will be in the box when he ventures out in Ireland's chilly mist, and his neighbor trusts that Coby will leave behind exactly what he owes.

Companies like GitHub,[7] which provides an online platform for collaborative software development, understand the importance of the Egg Principle. While the 313 full-time GitHub employees work primarily through remote teams, they perform a few defining rituals that maximize trust across the organization. One includes the entire company: an annual face-to-face gathering to reconnect with old colleagues and build new relationships. New hires are also required to spend a week at GitHub headquarters, where they get a feel for the organization's culture and meet key team members. But GitHub leaders are also skilled at building trust where face-to-face interactions are not possible. Example: employees are encouraged to shamelessly boast about their accomplishments on the company's internal messaging platforms. In response, their global teammates post selfies in which they raise a glass to acknowledge the success.

What can you learn about virtual teams from GitHub? To quote singing legend Stevie Wonder: "To know you is to love you." Basic human connections are the foundation of trust, which in turn is the foundation of teamwork. It just takes more work to build those connections in the virtual world. The key is to use a mixture of both digital and face-to-face trust-building mechanisms. Let's look at a few ways you can do this with your own team.

Build a Reciprocity Circle

To build trust, give and take.

The French sociologist Marcel Mauss[8] first noticed the power of give and take when he reviewed anthropological studies of gift-giving in cultures around the world. He anticipated finding dramatic differences between the gift-giving practiced by indigenous peoples like the Trobriand islanders of Papua, New Guinea, and the market-based transactions driving social relationships in his own city of Paris. But Mauss ended up confounding his own expectations. The decorative shells exchanged by islanders actually created long-term value, just like more complex transactions in the Paris Bourse. The only difference Mauss detected had to do with time. While market-based transactions were completed immediately, an islander, months after receiving a shell, might reciprocate by helping out with a neighbor's harvest.

The same principle of reciprocity applies in your world, as our Wharton colleague Adam Grant has shown in his best-selling book,[9] *Give and Take*. His research reveals that those who give generously—by supporting another's project, introducing someone to a new contact, or offering an expert opinion on a problem—tend to be the top performers in organizations. Why? Givers create a network of mutual support that they can draw on when they most need help. The more this type of giving occurs in a group, the more reciprocal bonds are created. The upshot: giving builds trust.

To jumpstart trust-building on virtual teams, we use a tool called the reciprocity circle (see Figure 5.1). Easily performed on a digital

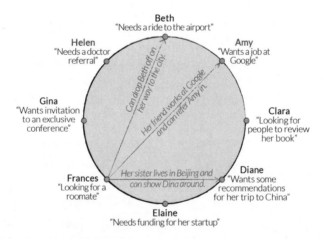

Figure 5.1   Reciprocity Circle

platform, this simple exercise models the give and take team members should practice on a regular basis.

Simply have people make requests of others either by email or on a shared group document. The requests can be about anything from connecting with someone in another area of your organization to getting help with a programming problem. Encourage people to respond to as many requests as they can.

You might be surprised at how much impact this basic exchange can have on relationships. One fortunate husband even used the circle to reignite the romance in his marriage. He had requested a reservation at a highly exclusive restaurant that provided him with the perfect setting to reconnect with his wife. We make no promises of successful couple's therapy, but we guarantee the reciprocity circle exercise will deepen the bonds of mutual commitment among your teammates, and that's no small feat.

The Water Cooler Goes Digital

Click!

The first thing we do in the morning is open our chat application, Slack. Our research has taught us the value of having an online hangout spot for teams and organizations. Slack functions like a virtual water cooler. Now we use it for all of our collaborations.

Among the early adopters of virtual water coolers like Slack (which we discuss at greater length further on) were groups like Philadelphia's Indy Hall. Founded in 2007, it was one of the first coworking spaces—open plan community offices that provide a home for the world's digital nomads: telecommuters, independents, freelancers, and entrepreneurs. These shared spaces create communities and opportunities. Members benefit from each other's wide range of perspectives, backgrounds, and expertise. Throughout the years, Indy Hall evolved through several virtual networking and communication platforms, utilizing the one that fits member needs at a given point in time. The virtual water cooler has been a fixture of the Indy Hall environment.

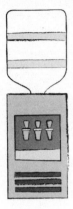
In any physical office, relationships are built not only in meetings but also between meetings. The virtual environment is no different. Around the virtual water cooler, you can discuss the previous night's episode of *Game of Thrones* or commiserate over the truly terrible coffee in the shared kitchen. In our years of studying virtual communities, coworking spaces, and so-called wide (dispersed across great geographic distances) teams, we have discovered several effective strategies for creating a virtual watercooler effect.

1. Make Socializing an Agenda Item   Make time during virtual meetings for teammates to catch up with each other. By formalizing this as an agenda item, you legitimize socializing and make it more likely that people will build trust-based relationships. Many of the folks we have interviewed dedicate the first 10 minutes of big virtual meetings to talking about shows they are watching or to ribbing each other about their fantasy football teams. This gives them a way to keep up the crucial rapport-building banter that happens naturally in face-to-face meetings, but can often be hard to initiate over a conference call.

2. Off-Topic Emails and Chat Rooms   It can be enervating when the only communication you have with your virtual team is the 100-email-long thread with the subject line: *Product Development Team—July Update*. Rapport is built through learning about each other's senses of humor, sharing quirky articles and videos, and celebrating successes that happen to occur outside of work. Early employees of GitHub were widely dispersed and recall:[10] "Chat was our office before we had a physical office." If you already have a chat platform, create a separate non-work-related channel or room. It can be a great place for hanging out. One team that we studied created a dedicated channel in their chat platform for sharing funny gifs (short, looped animated photographs, and videos).

3. More Frequent, Shorter Check-Ins   When your virtual team meets only once or twice a month on video, chat, or conference calls, the amount of work that needs to be done can build up and create stressful real-time discussions. By touching base more often—either by having more meetings, or communicating more frequently through chats—teams do better at staying in sync, emotionally and otherwise.

A Phone Call in Time Saves Nine

After a recent class, nine students clustered around us, with sheepish looks on their faces. Using our well-developed ESP, we suspected they wanted to talk about the assignment that was due the following week. Sure enough, one of them finally said: "We are behind schedule on our project."

We waited a moment. Another student piped up: "It's not really our fault. We emailed the client contact twice last week and they never got back to us!"

"Have you tried calling them?" we asked.

Blank stares. No matter that their project was falling well behind its time-line. Even to these high-achieving millennials, it seemed unfathomable that one should *pick up the phone and call someone*. It never occurred to them that their septuagenarian client actually prefers talking on the phone to exchanging emails.

The generational disconnect is a common one in virtual team communication. A CareerBuilder survey[11] of more than 3,800 full-time workers and more than 2,200 hiring managers found that only 10 percent of those aged 25 to 34 preferred to communicate by phone at work, defaulting to email and text instead. Oftentimes, their more senior colleagues wonder why they never call to get things done.

But the issue is bigger than generational divides. If you have ever wondered why a colleague called you back without checking the voicemail you left, or bristled at getting a text message instead of an email, you know that *how* you communicate with team members is as important as *what* you communicate to them. In the virtual world, you have to consider both the medium and the message. Virtual teams need to have internal check-ins, interface with external parties, share information, co-create and edit documents, brainstorm, and collectively make decisions, all without the face-to-face interactions that help them understand nuances of meaning and mood. Good communication is tough for any team, but the distance created by virtual teams makes it harder. Finding the right channels and setting ground rules for virtual communication become even more crucial to staying in sync.

Use Your Channels Wisely

New York Times journalists reach a global audience, yet these high-profile writers were having trouble communicating with colleagues in their own organization. Employees in Manhattan felt disconnected from co-workers stationed in other parts of the world, struggling to keep abreast of fast-moving stories in far-flung regions. Texts were ignored, emails languished in inboxes, and phone calls were tough to manage across international time zones. The Gray Lady was struggling with too many communication platforms to keep up with.

Remember Slack? We first mentioned it in our discussion about Indy Hall. It was a godsend for the *New York Times* journalists[12] who craved connecting with their colleagues. Of course, it may not fit your needs. But as you learn about how it helped the *Times,* consider what kind of chat channel works best for your virtual team.

Slack became wildly popular in 2014 and 2015. It is like Microsoft's Yammer, AOL's Instant Messenger (AIM), or the generic Internet Relay Chat (IRC). But Slack differs from those applications in that it is particularly well-suited for work teams. It archives messages, has a strong search engine, and allows for easy file sharing. It is also automatically synced across devices, and it promotes transparency and visibility in internal communications.

Slack's co-founder, Stewart Butterfield[13] designed it to boost employees' sense of connection to each other, no matter where they happen to be. "Being able to scroll back over the last couple weeks [in Slack messages], you get a whole bunch of 'soft knowledge' about how [a] company operates—how people relate to one another at this company, who knows the answers to most questions, who really makes the decisions," he claims.

After implementing Slack as an email replacement, the *New York Times* started to see the results. Tech columnist Farhad Manjoo has noticed the app's impact on his remote work:

"One danger of my job, as a columnist who works in California, is a feeling of disconnection from the mother ship in New York. Using Slack, I can peer into discussions that would never have been accessible to me. I can see how the producers and editors who are handling my column are discussing how to present it, and how the team overseeing the home page is thinking about my work. What's more, I have a feeling of intimacy with co-workers on the other side of the country that is almost fun. That's a big deal, for a job."

While Slack helped virtual teams at the *New York Times* feel closer together, some other channel may work better for your team. The last thing you want is "just another tool" that grows the mountain of messages you already receive from different media. So which channel is right for your virtual team and in what circumstances? The point is that you need to discuss this question. Choosing the right communication channel for different tasks is nearly as important as establishing your goals. In virtual space, miscommunication issues spread like an epidemic.

Questions for developing a Communications and Collaboration Platform

Selection

What do we need our tools to do?

What are the available options?

What tools are team members already using in their other work?

What capacity do team members have to learn new software?

Individual Communication Preferences

What is your order of preference for method of contact (email, phone call, text, chat message)?

What is your availability (when can I expect you to pick up the phone or respond to messages)?

When is off limits for phone calls?

Protocol

When do we use which tool?

What is our expectation for response times to emails, phone calls, texts, and chat messages?

What are our naming conventions for files and emails?

To determine what channels to use for different forms of collaboration, we recommend you create a communication protocol. You may decide that check-in meetings should happen over phone conferences, or can take place in the form of a weekly email chain. Short questions can be handled in a chat app or by videoconference. Whatever you decide, the ground rules should be determined up front and shared among the team.

A Note on Style and Tone

"I've been trying to reach out to u all day. r we still on for tonite?" Keegan aggressively taps into his phone.

"Aww, shoot, Keegan's been texting me," Peele mutters to himself, across town, when he puts down his video game controller and looks at his phone. He casually types his response: "Sorry, dude, missed your texts. I assumed we'd meet at the bar … whatever, I don't care."

"WHATEVER? … I DON'T CARE?" Keegan exclaims as he reads the message aloud.

Back and forth the exchange goes, Keegan more furious with each text until he has worked himself up into a fervor. Peele is clueless.

"You wanna go now?!" Keegan challenges Peele to a fight by text.

"Yeah, first round is on me!" Peele happily replies.

"Oh there aren't going to be any rounds, this is gonna be a street fight!" Keegan yells to himself as he exits his kitchen. He bursts into the bar ready to brawl, until Peele turns around on his barstool with a smile and says, "Oh! Bartender, a beer and a gimlet for my partner." As Keegan calms down, Peele cheerfully says, "Like I said, buddy, first round's on me!"

This is comedy—literally, from the *Key and Peele* show.[14] It beautifully illustrates a common problem that is no joke. It plagues virtual teams. You may think the message you sent to the team was an innocuous update, only to be overwhelmed by a torrent of electronic upset. Are others at fault for misinterpreting your meaning? Or did you cause the problem by not communicating more clearly?

Answer: Yes.

In a digital channel, it is impossible to capture all of the nuances of tone, cadence, rhythm, and body language packed into a face-to-face exchange. Sure, the advent of emoji may help. National Public Radio suggested[15] that "the increasingly abundant use of emojis across cultures and age groups—and the similar meanings we assign them—suggest we're entering an era of hybrid communication, as we treat pictures like a real language." But even in the pictorial realm of language there are differences in opinion about the meaning of a smiling cat emoji. In the United States versus China, or to a boomer versus a millennial, that feline appears sweet or surly. Same with that smiley face with its tongue sticking out—light-hearted greeting or insult?

To avoid these misunderstandings, virtual teams need guidelines for conveying and interpreting meaning in group messages, and give each other the benefit of the doubt. As in the Key and Peele sketch, the perceived difference between a friendly greeting and a hostile snipe can be razor thin in text or by email. High-performing virtual teams create guidelines to avoid crossing signals.

Where in the World Is My Teammate?

Have you ever tried to schedule transcontinental meetings verbally? It's harder than you think.

Let's check back with our GBI virtual team as they try to schedule the next call.

"Okay so if it's 3 P.M. my time, and you're … wait, how many hours ahead—err, no, behind are you? … okay so subtract 12, carry the 1, and … "

The problem? A consultant was going to be in New Zealand the day of the next meeting. Several people are on the U.S. East Coast, a few in California, one in London, and the other in Singapore. The back and forth needed to sort out time zones is maddening.

A major obstacle for global virtual teams is making dates to interact in real time. Although calendar applications help by translating the host's time zone for invitees, mistakes happen with surprising frequency. Ideally, you should take time at a kickoff meeting to schedule milestone reviews or recurring touchpoints. The sooner the team can solve the time zone puzzle, the better. Easier said than done, of course.

Another source of frustration is that global teams work asynchronously. Co-located teams have the benefit of proximity and synched time frames. You can count on your teammates being at work from approximately nine to five, around the corner from your office. Simple questions—"Hey, what does this number mean?"—can be answered quickly with a short walk down the hall.

On a global team, the person who can provide the answer you need to meet a client deadline might be enjoying a blissful sleep. Jason Fried and David Heinemeier Hansson, the founders of cloud computing company Basecamp,[16] recommend that you organize virtual work hours so that at least four hours overlap across time zones. In their organization, Copenhagen work hours run from 11 A.M.–7 P.M. and Chicago hours from 8 A.M. to 5 P.M. This adjustment helps keep the two key hub cities in sync.

Beating Asynchronicity

1 Establish deadlines in a standardized time zone

Saying "I'll have it done end of business tomorrow" is confusing to a team member on the other side of the world. Pick one standard time zone—align your calendar with the client, headquarters, or the majority of your teammates.

2 Build in extra time in case of emergency

Expect that you will need to do extra work because you were given a new draft in the middle of the night before your morning presentation. Expect that you will be unable to reach your colleague in Taiwan exactly when you need to. Expect that the file will be corrupted. In short, expect problems.

3 Update, Update, Update

At the end of your workday, send a status update to people who are waiting on deliverables from you. Updates reduce stress, even when a deadline is a week away. Updates can take the form of an email/report update or just a quick sentence in a chat application.

Another way to manage asynchronicity is to engineer the 24/7 availability of information. Basecamp team members link their proprietary tool with GitHub. Fried and Hansson explain: "All our code is available at all times to everyone, including change suggestions that can be discussed in slow time—over a couple of hours or days—as programmers comment on the thread." Shared files, calendars, chats, and emails help make all information available all the time—to everybody. This is the next best thing to being there.

When Virtual Teams Go Wrong

In February of 2013, Yahoo! CEO, Marissa Mayer, canceled all of the company's remote work programs.[17]

The news did not go over well. Employees felt that commitments made when they were hired had been violated. Feminists criticized Mayer for making a move that would disproportionately hurt women in their workforce. Silicon Valley tech companies decried it as backward thinking. Hundreds of articles dissected the choice and debated Mayer's decision to call Yahoo!'s troops home.

Ultimately, ending flexible work arrangements was a success for Yahoo! as it helped them regroup around a unified company culture. Does this mean that virtual teams are always a worse option? Not necessarily. In fact, Mayer's decision drives home the point that all teams need to regroup at key intervals to check in and get aligned. At Yahoo!, this failed to happen virtually, so Mayer decided to do the work of reflection and alignment in person. As Reses observed in her memo, "some of the best decisions and insights come from hallway and cafeteria discussions, meeting new people, and impromptu team meetings."

> **YAHOO!**
> PROPRIETARY AND CONFIDENTIAL INFORMATION—DO NOT FORWARD
>
> Yahoos,
>
> Over the past few months, we have introduced a number of great benefits and tools to make us more productive, efficient and fun. With the introduction of initiatives like FYI, Goals, and PB&J, we want everyone to participate in our culture and contribute to the positive momentum. From Sunnyvale to Santa Monica, Bangalore to Beijing — I think we can all feel the energy and buzz in our offices.
>
> To become the absolute best place to work, communication and collaboration will be important, so we need to be working side-by-side. That is why it is critical that we are all present in our offices. **Some of the best decisions and insights come from hallway and cafeteria discussions, meeting new people, and impromptu team meetings.** Speed and quality are often sacrificed when we work from home. We need to be one Yahoo!, and that starts with physically being together.
>
> Beginning in June, we're asking all employees with work-from-home arrangements to work in Yahoo! offices. If this impacts you, your management has already been in touch with next steps. And, for the rest of us who occasionally have to stay home for the cable guy, please use your best judgment in the spirit of collaboration. Being a Yahoo isn't just about your day-to-day job, it is about the interactions and experiences that **are only possible in our offices.**
>
> Thanks to all of you, we've already made remarkable progress as a company—and the best is yet to come.
>
> Jackie

Virtual Teams Pain Point
Communication. Virtual teams lack the traditional means of building rapport, establishing trust, and achieving alignment.

Teamwork Tip
Focus on building rapport quickly and consistently through carefully chosen tools and processes.

3x3 Spotlight
To anticipate and avoid communication misunderstandings:
1. Create a Digital Protocol as a part of your Team Commitments Charter.
2. Be explicit about any cultural differences that may affect style, tone, frequency, and meaning of communication.

Our basic point in this chapter is that, with the right communication platforms and norms, virtual teams can build trust-based relationships, have productive discussions and impromptu check-ins, and move work along just as well as any co-located team. But the reality is that electronic channels make it harder to stay in sync.

You can get work done in the cloud, but it takes a huge effort to keep your team on the same page. Bottom line: virtual teams need to bring more discipline to the 3x3 Framework.

6 No Time for Teamwork? Lessons from Startups

"Culture?"

The half-formed question hung in the air between the puzzled speaker and a room full of students. We were hosting Larry, a founder of three successful energy startups, as a guest lecturer in our seminar on corporate culture at the University of Pennsylvania. We had just asked the veteran entrepreneur what we thought was a simple warm-up question: How do you create a high-performing culture on a startup team?

Larry pondered the question, scratching a headful of curly locks. Having spent the previous night preparing for an upcoming board meeting, he looked more than slightly disheveled. "Well," he responded, "when you're in a startup you're going 100 miles an hour 24 hours a day. You don't really have time to think about your team culture."

Although we would dispute his point about culture, we think Larry is right about the pace of startup teams. When we think of the work ethic of successful founding teams, we imagine multiday, marathon coding sessions, 3 A.M. phone calls with suppliers halfway around the world, and sleepless nights crafting pitches for investors. We think of stories like that of the founders of Dollar Shave Club, a successful online grooming products company.[1] Their razor subscription service took off so quickly that the team found themselves frantically printing trash bags full of mailing labels and throwing them over the wall of their distributing warehouse just to keep up with demand.

Admittedly, it might seem odd to write about startups in a book on team process. How can you think about group dynamics when you're going 100 miles an hour just to keep the business alive?

Our answer is simple: You have to.

Co-founding Twitter taught Biz Stone[2] that he would have to find ways to shape team rules and behaviors while exponentially growing the social media messaging service. As he learned: "A culture is going to form whether you like it or not, and if you pay attention to it, you can craft something that makes the company stronger." As we will see, Stone realized that the company's success depended in large part on his team's ability to build in a reflection process during each major organizational transition.

Triaging Culture

After some discussion, Larry agreed that a team will inevitably develop its own culture. "I guess what makes a start up different is you have to do a lot of triage," he offered. Triage is an appropriate description. What separates startups from other teams is the lack of a well-developed organizational context. This simple fact shapes everything that gives startups open space to make their own decisions even as they dangle on the precipice of bankruptcy. Startups exist in an intense environment in which wild highs and lows are the norm. Teams are free to dream big, and make radical changes. Energy can be poured into a single idea, unfettered by the demands of other projects in a larger company.

Startup teams lack the resources of a larger company, too. And the comfort of knowing if a project fails you can return to your old job. Startup teams are a seatbelt-free roller coaster ride.

In this environment, reflection can go by the wayside. You may not have time for long corporate-style retreats to establish your culture, reflect, and adapt. Like a doctor in an emergency room with patients streaming in, you have to do triage to work on the most important points of your team process. While this is a permanent condition for many startups, almost every team will experience a time-crunch, when speed is of the essence and stepping back to reflect feels impossible. Precisely in these times, the key is to devote as much energy as you can to managing your team culture.

Persistence and Resilience Trump Product

In fact, we would argue that, while a business model is important to a start-up, its team culture matters even more. Why? Because in a VUCA (volatility, uncertainty, complexity, and ambiguity) environment, the best-articulated vision for your company is likely to be radically altered sooner or later. Only passion and commitment can pull you through the changes. Julie Livingston, a co-founder of the major startup incubator Y-Combinator,[3] reached this conclusion after interviewing 32 founders of successful companies: "I'd say determination is the single most important quality in a startup founder. If the founders I spoke with were superhuman in any way, it was in their perseverance."

Resilience matters, too. A resilient team tends to beat a great idea in determining startup success. We are reminded of the time Bill Maris, managing partner at Google Ventures, told us about the company's legendary shared doc, where any employee can submit any idea, big or small. Imagine having access to a massive document full of ideas generated by the thousands of bright minds of Google. What would you pay for it? According to Maris, if you said one dollar, it would still be a dollar too much. His point: great ideas are nearly worthless. Execution defines the difference between ideas that never become more than a scrawled Post-it note or a shared document and the ones that transform markets.

Of course, execution comes down to your team and your team-work process.

For this reason, we have found that the 3x3 Framework is still crucial in a time crunch. But we acknowledge that a modified process is needed—one that focuses on what we call "reflection triggers" rather than more elaborate steps. For startup teams, and other teams that need to move fast, we recommend focusing on two teamwork tasks: creating a culture of resilience, and identifying 3x3 checkpoints.

Building a Culture of Resilience

The packed room of NFL players stared toward the speaker at the front of the room with puzzled looks on their faces. It was as though they had just been told they needed to lose their next game. They had enjoyed entrepreneur Bob Morgan's presentation, but there was one part of it that seemed to stump many of them.

Finally, one of the players spoke up: "Are you saying we should put together a team before we even know what product we want to make?"

In fact, that was exactly what Morgan was suggesting. His accomplishments included building a media-data aggregation tool called Sportstream, which had been acquired by Facebook. A year later, he addressed our group as a member of Facebook's media partnerships team in a crowded conference room on the company's sunny Menlo Park campus. The players were there as part of a Wharton program designed to help them build business skills for post-football careers. They were visiting with entrepreneurs like Morgan to learn more about the ins and outs of founding a successful business. Morgan was causing the aspiring business founders to rethink everything they had assumed about creating a startup.

Morgan explained that even if they had a great idea for a product or service, they would need a good team to help them further flesh out, refine, and implement the idea. Even then, they would likely change the focus of their product, or maybe reinvent the product itself multiple times as they received feedback from the market. People therefore came before product, as they did with Morgan's own Sportstream. That venture was itself an offshoot of the Paul Allen–backed news aggregator Evri, where Morgan had been an executive.

In forming a startup team, a general rule we have heard over and over from successful entrepreneurs is to find good co-founders before worrying about the fine details of your offering. You may not even have a vague idea for what that offering is when you create the team.

Take Joe Kraus,[4] who in the early 1990s reached out to five of his friends at Stanford about starting a venture together. Joe had no clue what they were going to do, he just knew that these people were so talented that he had to work with them. As he recounts, "We decided to start a company together before we had any idea what we were going to work on. But we were so committed to the idea of starting something together that we knew we were going to figure it out." The group of college buddies headed to a nearby taqueria, where they threw out bad idea after bad idea, until something seemed to stick: a tool for searching the universe of digital information, which at that time was expanding at an unwieldy rate.

The original product was intended for databases. But as the company began to gel in 1994, Kraus and his friends turned their attention to a newer source of digital information with massive growth potential: the web. The team focused on creating an online index that would become Excite—one of the first search engines. Between the creation of an idea for an indexing tool to the emergence of a leading search engine company, there were plenty of pivots, but the team's resilience enabled the fledgling operation to navigate each twist and turn.

Building a culture of resilience begins with the raw material of your teammates: whom you select and how you deploy them. This is true not only for co-founders. As we explain in the next section, it applies to the extended "team," as well.

Prioritize Talent Management over Tasks

Are your team members Walters or Douglases?[5] This is the question Marty Seligman, a University of Pennsylvania professor and pioneer of positive psychology might ask. In Seligman's telling, both Walter and Douglas are Wharton MBAs who are let go by their Wall Street firms. Walter takes the hit hard. He questions his abilities and spirals into depression, never fully recovering from the blow. Douglas bounces back and is more determined than ever to succeed. He sees the failure as a learning opportunity and uses it to self-develop while pushing his career forward. Walter and Douglas are archetypes of the people Seligman has encountered in his work: those who wilt in difficult moments versus those who display resilience in the face of failure.

One way to create a culture of resilience is to simply hire Douglas types, like Austin Geidt who worked her way up through the car-sharing company Uber.[6] She was fresh out of school, a talented bright young graduate in a dismal job market, when she reached out to the young company's CEO. When Ryan Graves interviewed Geidt, he didn't have a specific role in mind for her but he saw promise in her intelligence and proactive nature. He decided to bring her on as an intern. At first, Geidt would do anything and everything the team needed to grow. In an interview with *Fortune,* she describes the odd jobs she took on, ranging from handing out flyers to taking customer service calls personally in the middle of the night.

While it was tough to float around, she found any way to add value that she possibly could, proving her ability to adapt to new challenges on the fly. She began to define herself as a customer relations guru until the employee in charge of managing driver relations moved on, leaving her with that role as well. Geidt was a quick study, paying attention to every detail of the process for launching Uber in a new city. She noted improvements along the way: when she saw that a new driver in the company's limo service was driving a pink minivan, she recommended a vehicle check system. Geidt's talent and tenacity led her to eventually develop a unique expertise in the launch process. Within two years of joining Uber as an intern, she was named head of global expansion.

Geidt wasn't hired for a particular role. She was hired for her talent and persistence. The team defined and redefined her role as the company developed.

When picking the members of your startup team, therefore, prioritize bringing people on board who have proven that they are able to drive doggedly toward fulfilling a vision, even if they have to completely change how they approach it in the process. Take note of those who proactively reach out as Geidt did. Probe them in interviews on how they have responded to setbacks. Watch for red flags, such as blaming others rather than focusing on what they did to adjust. Forget about their past failures. Focus on what they learned from them.

Hiring to fill specific roles is secondary. Like your product, chances are team roles will change, dramatically. Any role you hire for may become obsolete. What does not become obsolete is a team member who can adapt and learn a new set of tasks on the job. Just like Geidt.

Another way to fill your team with these Douglas types is to culti-vate them. Seligmann has dedicated decades to understanding how to build resilience. It turns out that a big part of the answer has to do with self-awareness. People like Douglas understand their own strengths and focus on leveraging them to get through tough moments rather than mitigating weaknesses.

Whether she knew it or not, Geidt was playing to her strengths in relationship-building and process-management as she jumped from role to role, building expertise and experience along the way. A more structured way to do this is to have your team members explore their own strengths and take up roles that play to those strengths. Selig-mann's own values-in-action survey is a great place to start reflecting on strengths. The tool is available free at viacharacter.org.

On startups or any team on which speed becomes a priority, hiring and cultivating resilient people ensures you have the right raw materials in place to manage the resulting pressure. When forming your team, focus on this form of talent management rather than hiring for tasks. The right roles will emerge.

Build a Network of Champions

Richard Hackman saw organizational support as a key success factor for teams. Any team needs external resources and outside perspectives to grow and adapt. This is true for startups, even though they lack this organizational resource base. Successful startup teams compensate by cultivating a robust network of external relationships.

What Kraus calls the "six smart friends" who started Excite were talented enough to create a great product, but they needed the support of legendary Silicon Valley investor Vinod Khosla to weather potentially catastrophic setbacks. This Kleiner-Perkins partner pushed them to take risks they would not have otherwise had the appetite for, and gave them the advice they needed to succeed. As Kraus details, Excite faced a critical juncture when there was an opportunity to become the embedded search tool for Netscape, which at the time was one of the dominant Internet browsers on the market. The problem: with $1 million in the bank, Excite didn't have nearly enough to win the bid.

Khosla encouraged the company to bid $3 million, explaining: "If we win, I'm pretty sure we can raise it, but if we don't win, I don't know how we're going to raise it." Terrified, Kraus and his friends bid $3 million, only to still lose to another competitor, MCI. Khosla advised them to not take no for an answer and to keep meeting with the Netscape people, showing up at their offices unannounced if need be. The tactic paid off when it turned out MCI couldn't build the tool as promised, and Netscape turned to Excite for the contract. Kraus credits this development with saving the company.

As an investor, Khosla provided the financial resources and the Silicon Valley wisdom needed to keep the startup on track. The sheer amount of time he spent advising Kraus was unusual, and a testament to the strength of their relationship. Kraus's team needed that kind of external champion to thrive. As you build your own startup team, think about the people you need inside the company as well as the champions you need in your external network. All startups need a supportive social ecosystem to survive.

These relationships can be developed and nurtured formally, through networking events, conferences, and informational interviews. They can also develop in unexpected ways. Y-Combinator partner Michael Seibel and co-entrepreneur Justin Kan once let three new friends stay at their apartment.[7] Michael had just met them at the SXSW music and media festival. As one of the friends would later recount: "We were these crazy people, three guys with three airbeds in the living room. People thought this [i.e. their business model] was the worst idea. They were the only people, I think, who believed in us." Despite many investors thinking the would-be founders' service would never fly, Seibel introduced them around and eventually helped them get funding through Y-Combinator.

Who were the three "crazy guys?" The founders of Airbnb, now one of the most successful companies ever launched through Y-Combinator. Seibel had no idea he was dealing with the future leaders of a multibillion-dollar company, but he had the instinct to build his network and help others. He says the support he provided them has paid dividends many times over as they have given him even greater recognition and made excellent referrals for his incubator.

Research on social capital shows that those who have more of it tend to be seen as more competent, get promoted more quickly, and earn more. Social capital is valuable for startups, too. Teams with more and stronger connections are more likely to avail themselves of the advice and funding relationships they need at crucial junctures.

When you are building your extended "team," aim to fill three vital roles in particular:

1. **Supporters:** These are people like Khosla who can give you the financial resources or technical support you need to accomplish your goals.

2. **Advocates:** Like Seibel, advocates are believers in your mission who are willing to go to bat for you with skeptics and open doors for you with potential supporters when need be.

3. **Advisers:** These are third-party experts in your team's field who can help you polish your ideas and recommend course corrections when you run into barriers.

Some people may fill all three of these roles, as Khosla did for the Excite team. The point is to have a diverse network of contacts who collectively fill these needs. This larger team provides your go-to resources when time is tight. The network also supports your culture of resilience.

Create 3x3 Checkpoints

What makes it even harder for many startup teams to stop and reflect is they think they don't need to. Teams tend to be close-knit. Typical ones evolve from groups of friends and work together more consistently than teams in large organizations. Because of this closeness, start-up teams tend to fall into the trap of believing that everyone is in sync and that they can focus on executing without spending time thinking about alignment.

Dangerous assumption. In the fast-paced start-up world, teams that fail to check on their process often experience disconnects that cause problems such as product misfires and missed milestones. This was one of Biz Stone's major takeaways from his startup experience: "I've learned that lack of communication is what usually causes a startup to fail. Our company is only seven people right now, and we're all in the same room, so it's easy to assume that we're all on the same page. But we're not—I have to work to make sure we get there, even if I spend 50 percent of my time communicating."

But how you stay in sync on team process when speed is the priority? Whether you are in a startup or on an organization-based team in a time crunch, you need checkpoints. Rather than thinking of the 3x3 Framework all the time, you should create predetermined triggers that lead to specific actions, such as a meeting or a decision-point. You should focus your reflection on only the most important adjustments that drive passion and performance on your team, and you should make them automatic actions that you initiate only when the right conditions arise.

We recommend establishing checkpoints for three types of team issues:

1. Checking the participation and engagement of individual team members
2. Flagging problems as they arise
3. Making pivots when necessary

Participation Checkpoints: Create the Ground Rules

Startup teams are unique in that many are created among circles of friends, like the Excite founders who just knew that they had to work together. These teams grapple with a tough question: Is it a good idea to do business with your buddies? Tim Brady faced this dilemma[8] when he mulled an offer by his old college friend Jerry Yang to become the first employee at Yahoo!. He was so excited about the company that he arranged to graduate from Harvard Business School a semester early so that he could rush out to California.

But first he had to consider whether it was a good idea to work with someone who had been so close to him. What enabled Brady to take the leap was a conversation with Yang that helped them separate professional decisions from their personal relationship: "So one of the things that really helped me was that he and I had a conversation before I joined, 'Okay, here are the ground rules.' And this is really what made me think about it. 'Okay, if this happens, I walk away.' We had the conversation in order to preserve our friendship, having no idea what was going to happen, but that conversation got me thinking about it and why was I involved."

One of the biggest mistakes startup teams make is to assume that they can just work out conflicts as they arise because the members all know each other. In fact, the close personal relationships can make tough business decisions all the more difficult to talk about in the open. By establishing "ground rules," Tim and Jerry were able to come to a clear understanding of the terms of Tim's involvement in the company, his reasons for being there, and what would cause him to break the commitment. Creating these agreements makes it easier for everyone to buy in to a transition or a founder's exit when the time comes.

When you bring in team members, create checkpoints that flag major decisions about their level of involvement in the startup. If they are only with the startup part time to begin with, what would make them go full time, and how will you know when you have reached that moment? What would cause them to leave the company? The answers to these questions become your checkpoints that trigger discussions around promotions, firings, or divestments.

Problem Checkpoints: Raise the Yellow Flag

Another aspect of communicating well is to know when to slow down and raise a "yellow flag." The term comes from athlete-turned-entrepreneur, Jeremy Bloom.[9] Bloom believed that his marketing company Integrate was hitting snags in part because he and his co-founder were not on the same page about when to take risks. His partner had a driver-like communication style and didn't pick up on Jeremy's subtler cues about feeling discomfort with a big decision. Even when he would express apprehension, Jeremy found that his partner would misinterpret his level of seriousness.

When Jeremy had finally had enough of feeling like his input was ignored, he came up with a rating system for "yellow flags"—points of caution before proceeding. The partners would put a number on their level of discomfort with a decision or pressing issue from 1 to 10. Sometimes, Jeremy felt mildly unsure of a decision, but not enough to block it. Other times he would say: "This one is an 8 for me. We need to reconsider." Their system was based on a clear, easy-to-understand way to raise discomfort. As startups move quickly and the stakes are high, assessing your team's appetite for risk regularly is crucial to keeping them aligned with major decisions. Having a quick and easy way to deal with discomfort is a necessary process tool.

Checkpoints create mechanisms to generate buy-in for things that are likely to be key areas of tension on your team, such as decisions about bringing in new investors and team members, or changing product features. Simple ideas like Bloom's comfort scale reading or a 15-minute stand-up meeting are effective ways to ensure your teammates are in sync. Checkpoints are essential for raising uncomfortable issues and help prime your team to take risks and experiment.

Pivot Checkpoints: Prepare to Fail

The final set of checkpoints should address the one event that every startup is guaranteed to experience—the all-important pivot, when you change your offering as you learn more about customer needs. This transition hopefully takes your company to the next level, but it is inevitably preceded by failure. Failure is a way of life in startups. The key is having a clear sense of when to decide on a pivot and what information will help you set a new direction.

The difference between a pivot and bankruptcy is timing. In 2010, Pinterest founder Ben Silbermann was low on capital.[10] His original app idea—Tote—failed to catch on, and he questioned the decision to

Teams Triggers and 3x3 Actions
Participation
Example: Roles begin diverging from self-identified strengths
We hold a meeting to realign team members' tasks
Problems
Example: We make a major change to product design
Each founder gives a 1 - 10 "comfort rating" on proceeding
Pivots
Example: We miss a sales target for a new product line two quarters in a row
We make a decision on divesting from that product

leave his job at Google. Tote was supposed to disrupt the entire remote shopping experience, replacing paper catalogues with online versions that made clothing easy to browse, wish-list, and purchase. Snags with the mobile payment system dampened user growth, and Silbermann was now looking wistfully at his friends who were still working at Google, enjoying free drinks and a steady paycheck.

He noticed that while people weren't signing up for Tote in droves, the ones who did join were fanatical about one part of the app, a minor feature that let them "pin" and share clothes they loved with their friends. Silbermann made the pivot and relaunched his product with that single feature at its core. The site was called Pinterest, and just two years after its launch it was drawing 20 million unique visitors per month and being pegged with a $1.5 billion valuation.

Silbermann could have continued tinkering with Tote and run out of capital. Indeed, there are more Totes than Pinterests in the world of startups. The difference between the two is knowing when to persevere and when to switch course. Also important is being able to keep your team on the same page about the decision. The key to identifying pivot checkpoints and maintaining team alignment through the shift is to have clear metrics. What is your measure of success and how long do you allow your team to fail to hit the mark before changing?

Knowing the answer to this question will enable you to adapt and experiment rapidly to hook customers before your cash flow runs dry. The success of Kodak Gallery as a photo sharing service[11] is a testament to the power of clear road signs pointing the way toward perseverance or change. When Vice President of Products Mark Cook set out to create the service, he had his team develop clear hypotheses from the beginning about why and how customers would want to use such a service. They began with the basic assumption that customers would want to share photo albums from specific events.

Early users clamored to the site, eager to share wedding and conference photos. But no one was able to create an album and many complained about the scarcity of features. Many entrepreneurs would have pulled back at this point—if no one is creating event albums on a site made to share event albums, isn't the product a failure? But because the team had identified a clear metric in advance—user interest in creating such albums—they were able to see beyond the setback and identify a pivot opportunity. They had confirmed that customers would come to the site if it were more user-friendly. This clear metric of interest also helped Cook persuade higher-ups (think of them as his investors) to give him more time to sort out the product design. In the efficiency-oriented culture of Kodak, this was huge. The revamped site ended up building a base of 75 million users before being sold to Shutterfly in 2012.

What are your pivot checkpoints? With your team, identify the key assumptions driving your product idea and determine a metric, whether it be unique visitors to a site, number of social media shares, or customer ratings. Then, just as important, determine a timeline for persevering or pivoting based on those metrics. At what point will you reconvene and go a different route or what mark do you have to hit to deem the product a success? Creating this clarity will keep your team and company stakeholders aligned as you push forward and pivot on the road map to growth.

Culture on the Fly

Entrepreneur Eric Ries lays out a "lean startup" process in his now-classic book of the same name that is considered required reading at GE and other leading companies. Why the intense focus on process? As Ries explains, it is impossible to anticipate all contingencies in a startup—the plan will constantly change. What you can do is create the right culture and habits so that when challenges emerge, your team knows how to react. As he notes, the popular photo-sharing site Flickr started as an online game. What enabled them to make the necessary radical shifts was a good process for determining when to move forward with a product and when to make a clear "pivot."

What is true for startups is true for any team for which speed is the priority. A process is needed that maximizes adaptability. While the 3x3 Framework is a foundation for any successful team, triage is

Startup Team Pain Point
Speed. Startup teams are constantly in crisis mode.
Teamwork Tip
Even when speed is a team's primary concern, make time for reflection.
3x3 Spotlight
To maintain situational awareness, focus on:
1. Cultivating a culture of resilience
2. Build in checkpoints

key in this intense environment. Creating a culture of resilience and setting 3x3 checkpoints are the best mechanisms for keeping your team on track and ready to move with the wild swings of startup growth. The important thing is to not triage team culture out altogether.

7 Who Has a Good Idea? Insights on Innovation

L ouis C.K. is about to experience first-hand[1] how an innovative team solves a high-stakes problem. But for the moment he is focused solely on his own *Saturday Night Live* monologue. Having practiced delivering 12 minutes of material, he is hell-bent on using every last second of it.

In an interview with his friend Judd Apatow, a leading Hollywood comedy writer and movie director, C.K. later recounted training for the solo performance "in really shitty places" where he was sure to be playing "without any support" before small, completely uninterested audiences. He was testing himself under the toughest conditions. He had never worked so hard, and the piece got steadily better week by week. At the *SNL* dress rehearsal, C.K. boasted, he "f---ing killed."

Just afterward, he feels "jacked up" as he heads into a meeting with Lorne Michaels, *SNL*'s revered creator and producer, who wants to discuss the imminent televised performance. Settling into an oversized leather chair, C.K. remembers his manager's advice: "Don't let Lorne cut a single minute."

Michaels has other ideas. "So you did 12 minutes in the monologue," he says. "How much do you want to do on-air?"

"I want to do all 12," C.K. replies.

"You're not doing 12. It was good but there was a lot of air in it, a lot of stopping and starting."

Red-faced, C.K. shoots back, "I'm doing 12."

"Calm down," Michaels tells him. "I'll you give you seven and nobody's ever done seven."

Show time is rapidly approaching. "I want to see the monologue from rehearsal," C.K. demands. An exasperated Michaels asks one of his writers to let C.K. see the tape. He is shocked. "*It's not that good,*" C.K. thinks. He agrees to let one of the *SNL* writers help him cut the material.

In reflecting on that experience, C.K. recalled a comment made by Amy Poehler, an *SNL* regular and friend: "Just give yourself to the process." Lorne Michaels and his team of writers had spent years refining that process. It could only make Louis C.K., already at the top of his game, even better.

Innovation Takes Work

Louis C.K.'s story illustrates three key findings from the research on innovation:

1. *It requires discipline*. Like other accomplished comedians, creative artists, and professionals of all kinds, Louis C.K. is a disciplined practitioner. He constructs an act piece by piece, testing jokes to see if they get a laugh, tweaking the ones that do, and discarding those that fall flat. Fellow comedian-great Jerry Seinfeld says he employs "trial and error," always "trying new material." Seinfeld attributes his extraordinary success to the fact that he "works harder than most other people." Inspiration seems to have little to do with their innovative performances.

2. *It depends on social interaction*. As the writer Steve Johnson puts it, new ideas are rarely created in "glorious isolation."[2] They often

emerge from intensely social environments, like cities, research centers, teams, and partnerships. When people talk and write to each other, they innovate in ways that individuals working alone seldom do. Without that tense conversation with Lorne Michaels, for example, Louis C.K. would not have recognized that his monologue would be much better if it were a few minutes shorter.

3. *It can be learned*. Innovation is a deliberate, painstaking activity, and your team can study and practice it. It bears little resemblance to the "flash of insight" occurrences that are the fanciful stuff of popular legend. Most likely, that apple never did fall on Isaac Newton's head. So forget about having such a fruit-inspired moment with your team. You should get used to the idea of working hard at innovation, like the *SNL* team. Creativity relies on a well-managed process.

Innovation is an activity that teams need to perform all the time—in designing a new product or service, adapting a business model to a changing market, troubleshooting a technical glitch, or doing any task that requires creativity. Worried that your teammates are deficient in that department? Follow Jerry Seinfeld's lead and work harder to help them develop the necessary habits that promote innovation.

Innovation Principles and Kickstarters

We have learned that innovative team cultures have a few distinctive habits. You can help your teammates develop those habits by asking the right questions. We call them "kickstarters." They will enhance the way you solve problems, conduct meetings, and collaborate with people outside the team. The result: closing the saying-doing gap that frequently exists in innovation-related work.

You want to be innovative? Here is how you really do it. Each of the following sections includes a "kickstarter" question that you can put on the agenda of your next team meeting about innovation.

Define Values

Innovative companies and teams are committed to values that every-body takes seriously. Values are like guardrails that keep ideas from veering off the path leading to core goals.

Alice Waters, founder of the world-renowned Chez Panisse[3] restaurant and a major figure in the California Cuisine movement, knows exactly what she and her team value: food that is "season-able, local, organic, and sustainable." Since the early 1970s, this well-defined value has guided choices about the farmers and suppliers who provide the raw ingredients used in the kitchen and the dishes that appear on the daily menu. Over time, the Chez Panisse team has developed a thriving ecosystem of people and organizations that exchange ideas about agriculture, high end dining, and social responsibility.

Early innovations included the practice of "hunting and gathering" in local supermarkets and stores and even streams and roadsides, at a time when chefs at the most expensive restaurants were using frozen meats and vegetables. Waters wanted her team members to have a "hands-on understanding of where food comes from"—what better way to promote that understand-ing than having people foraging out in the wild for the evening's offer-ings? She also encouraged patrons and chefs from other restaurants to wander into the kitchen to share ideas and make suggestions. Because she and her team have remained true to their fundamental values, they know how to pick and choose among all of the innovative ideas this inclusiveness produces.

Like the Chez Panisse team, IKEA employees are knowledgeable about what the company stands for.[4] Many stores display an image of a stone wall as a reminder of the region where its Swedish founder, Ingvar Kamprad, was raised. Largely agricultural and poor, Smaland imbued Kamprad with an appreciation for innovative frugality. This value has driven the creation of myriad well-designed products, including a table that can be sold at a profit for five euros. At first glance, the very idea might seem impossible to realize. Five euros? At a profit? Given the challenge of developing a prototype that met these specifications, team members networked with colleagues across the company and reached out to suppliers. The exploration led to an improbable source: door manufacturers. Cut a door in two—presto! You have a table. In retrospect, this makes perfect sense. But it took creative thinking to get there.

DARPA, the Pentagon's Defense Advanced Research Projects Agency, has a long history of forming teams[5] that have produced innovations such as the Internet, drones, and GPS. One of the reasons DARPA has been able to deliver results for decades is its clear commitment to combining basic and applied research. Many university departments pursue pure science, while R&D departments in for-profit companies focus mostly on practical application. By contrast, DARPA looks for ways to apply new scientific discoveries to emerging practical problems. This orientation expresses a value. It also guides decisions in a high priority area: the selection of projects, such as recent ones in cyber security and microelectro mechanical systems. The problems that need to be solved in these fields require a unique kind of creativity and teamwork. DARPA teams combine a grasp of cutting-edge science with an anthropologist's appreciation for user needs. How many R&D groups can boast of such a capability?

Bottom line: a team that has committed to a well-defined set of values knows how to spend its creative energy. Just as important, it also knows how *not* to spend it. The diverse examples of Chez Panisse, IKEA, and DARPA show why teams innovate best when they know what defines their identity. They avoid brainstorming-type discussions that only drain energy and waste time on abstract possibilities. They know what kinds of problems deserve their attention and avoid getting distracted by the next big thing.

Do you notice an attribute that characterizes every example we have discussed so far? Innovators of all kinds—chefs, product

Innovation Kick-Starter: Define Values
What does our team stand for, and how is that reflected in
the problems we work on?

designers, applied
research specialists,
performing artists—
are *focused*. Of course,
they have other attributes, too. Some, like the ability to see a problem
from multiple perspectives, might seem very different, even contradictory. But we think innovation has an underlying structure that causes
these varied attributes to enhance and reinforce each other. We explain
why in the following sections of this chapter.

Multiply Perspectives

Values help orient your team and guide exploration of multiple perspectives on a problem. Innovative teams encourage this sort of pur-
poseful yet wide-ranging inquiry. There are several ways to do it.

One way is to read—voraciously, widely, and intensely. Bill Gates
takes reading vacations,[6] laying aside a diverse collection of books for
most of the year and quickly working through them during a one- or
two-week binge. When you immerse yourself in this way, you make
connections that are harder to see when you read more slowly and
forget details. (Of course, it is best to read all the time, but the reality
of busy schedules often gets in the way.) Some of our clients have
organized reading groups and each month discuss a book about some
business-related topic or even one that transports team members to an
exotic locale, like the world of philosophy or neuroscience.

Alice Waters creates an environment that promotes learning. She
pays her chefs to visit local farmers markets and even to travel in
search of innovative culinary ideas. Chefs can also take four months
off, at full pay, to work as teachers in cooking schools. Patricia Curtan,
Chez Panisse's menu designer, recognizes the value of stepping back
from the day-to-day pressure of working: "Some of the very best chefs
say you have to get away for a while and go do something. They
learn a bunch and get inspired and come back full of ideas. It's like
taking a mini-sabbatical." Not surprisingly, chefs and other employees
sometimes leave this intense learning environment and go on to start
their own businesses or work for other restaurants. At first, Waters

was unhappy with the departures, but eventually she started to see them differently.[7] Her friend Mary Canales, founder of Ici Ice Cream, explains: "Alice once told me years ago that she had a hard time with people leaving, and when they left, she was upset. Later she said 'It's kind of like a school' and that she would train them and send them out in the world." T. McNamee, author of *Alice Waters and Chez Panisse*, thinks the school-like atmosphere promotes innovation: "[Alumni chefs] return with new experience and valuable ideas. In this way Chez Panisse fertilizes the wider world of restaurants and is fertilized in turn."

You might think that only a relatively small operation like Chez Panisse could open itself up so fully, but corporate behemoths such as IBM and AT&T[8] manage to encourage cross-fertilization on a grander scale. IBM organizes "jams," using the web to facilitate high energy interactive discussions involving thousands of employees. Topics run the gamut from business strategy to programming. AT&T invites customers to spend time at its foundries, like tourists visiting another country. Mondelez International, a global food concern, brings customers to a dedicated innovation space called the Fly Garage. There, innovation specialists team with customers, quickly prototype ideas, and assess real-time reactions. One of the specialists comments: "That is amazing, because we then get to look into the faces of the real people and ask what they like and what they'd change."

Companies that treat customers like a team member generate insights that shape innovative products and services. The founders of Hotmail, a web-based email service,[9] used a customer insight to shape its wildly successful business model. An important aspect of the model was based on nudging customers to make a small behavioral change: moving their email from the desktop to the web. In 1996, many people were already comfortable working with computers and accustomed to surfing the web. Given that, setting up a Hotmail account was easy: enter your name at the site, choose a password, and provide a little bit of demographic information. One of the founders observed: "If you are expecting people to dramatically change the way they do things, it's not going to happen. Try to make it such that it's a small change, yet an important one."

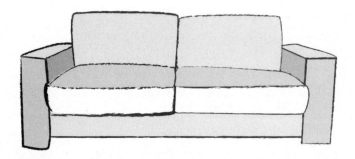

Product developers at IKEA have found that just talking with customers is not enough. Sometimes you have to live with them. Research leader Mikael Ydholm says:[10] "Sometimes we are not aware about how we behave, and therefore we say things that maybe are not the reality." Company anthropologists travel to Milan, New York, and Shenzhen to move in with customers. Surprising things are discovered. In Shenzen, people sat on the floor of their apartments and used sofas as backrests. Ydholm told a reporter: "I can tell you seriously we for sure have not designed our sofas according to people sitting on the floor and using a sofa like that."

At Procter & Gamble, CEO A.G. Lafley launched[11] an initiative called Connect + Develop to multiply the perspectives that corporate executives, scientists, and R&D specialists were considering. The initiative built relationships with technology entrepreneurs, university professors, and C-suite-level business leaders at other corporations. The outreach has produced new products like the Crest Spinbrush and Olay Regenerist. In the early 2000s, a third of all new products came from Connect + Develop.

Our Wharton colleagues Christian Terwiesch and Karl Ulrich[12] propose that you use "innovation tournaments" to multiply perspectives. The basic structure is simple: contestants (people or ideas) compete with one another in a series of elimination rounds and eventually just a few survivors—the most valuable ones—remain. Sound competitive? You bet it is. Terwiesch and Ulrich celebrate this aspect of the highly structured process. They have even created an innovation management software tool called the "Darwinator." You can run an innovation tournament with literally thousands of people, or just with your team and a few clients or customers. Participants generate ideas, which are then filtered by voting or some other method such as the application of a template that assesses profitability or feasibility. Most of us are familiar with a popular version of an innovation tournament: *American Idol*. On the original televised talent show that spawned numerous imitators, thousands of performers experienced the exhilaration or humiliation of being publicly judged by juries around the country. They waited in line for hours and sweat bullets in hopes of reaching the final televised round. In the end, one winner stood alone on the stage. As Terwiesch and Ulrich put it bluntly: "Many contestants compete, but only the fittest survive."

Whether you are partial to reading, sabbaticals, prototyping, or competing, you have many choices when it comes to multiplying perspectives on a problem or opportunity. We have suggested a few options, but you should choose the one that feels right for your team. What works depends on your team's values and culture. But one basic point applies to all teams: innovators seek out multiple perspectives. Recent research shows that the human mind tends to become fixed in how it thinks about people and objects. Many innovation techniques are designed to overcome precisely this "functional fixity"[13] that many studies have analyzed. One way to do it is exposing your team to unfamiliar perspectives (see Figure 7.2). We have no doubt that you will like the process as well as the results.

> *Innovation Kick-Starter: Multiply Perspectives*
> How can we multiply perspectives on the problem we want to solve?

Tinker

Let's assume that you have used one or two of the ideas we just discussed to create lots of ideas for a new product or service, a business model, or a solution to a seemingly intractable problem. What's next? Tinkering. Innovators tinker—or, in other words, they experiment.

Innovation is messy. While you can use a highly structured activity like a tournament to generate ideas, the core process of creating a new product, a strategy, a novel, or a symphony is always iterative.

It happens in fits and starts. It involves serendipity. It requires that your team members listen to themselves think out loud, babbling half-sentences and nonsense.

At this point, we imagine you might be feeling confused. "Wait," you say. "First you tell me to define my team's values. Okay, did that. Then I used an innovation tournament to generate lots of ideas, just like you suggested. That produced a bunch of ideas that align with my team's values. Now you want me to babble and tinker?"

That's right. At the very least, we want you to tinker. Because the innovation research shows that good ideas are cobbled together in just this way. You reach the same conclusion when you read about how creative people—artists, scientists, strategists, political leaders—actually produce their ideas. They do it little by little, experiencing equal amounts of confusion, disappointment, and passion.

A hilarious skit done by the British comedy troupe Monty Python[14] shows how wrong-headed it is to think that good ideas are produced in any other way. Imagine the nineteenth-century novelist Thomas Hardy—whose book *Far From the Madding Crowd* was recently cinematized—sitting down at a desk in the middle of a huge stadium full of screaming fans. A commentator breathlessly narrates the actions. Hardy picks up his pen. The crowd roars. Hardy puts down his pen. The crowd boos. Hardy picks up his pen and writes the word "The." The crowd goes wild. Hardy crosses out the word. The crowd emits a collective groan. And so on—for four minutes. You get the idea: Absurd. But so many popular accounts of creativity seem to assume it is or should be a linear process. Of course, Thomas never wrote that way, and no innovator actually produced a new idea that way.

More realistic is the way actual innovators describe the creative process. Consider what the novelist John Gregory Dunne said in an interview[15] with an editor from *The Paris Review*:

> I think any time a writer tells you where a book starts, he is lying, because I don't think he knows. You don't start off saying, "I'm going to write this grand saga about the human condition." It's a form of

accretion. . . . When I am between books I am an inveterate note taker. I jot things down mainly because they give me a buzz. I like to go to the library and take a month's newspaper, say August of 1962, and read through it. You can find great stuff in those little filler sections at the bottom of a page. Then when it comes time to start writing a book, I sort of look through the stuff and see if any of it works.

Dunne takes notes about things that give him buzz, things for which he has some passion. We suggest you have your team members do the same and follow their bliss—*after,* that is, you have defined values and generated multiple perspectives on a problem. If you go for the buzz without doing the other work, all you end up with is a buzz. But no good ideas.

We have seen many examples already of the process that produces ideas that work. Louis C.K. was tinkering when he slipped off to small clubs to test out the *SNL* monologue he was developing. For years, Jerry Seinfeld has used trial and error to create new jokes that people find funny. You might recall that Steve Martin was always refining his material by putting himself in odd, challenging situations, like the one where he gave a performance in a crowded classroom with columns that obstructed the view of many audience members. That experience taught Martin something new—the power of responding flexibly to real time to situational factors affecting his live performances. That insight helped make him a superstar.

But what if your team is running a business—a big one like a television network? The same principle of small-scale experimentation applies. Consider the challenge facing Kent Alterman at Comedy Central.[16] As president of content and original programming, Alterman has to figure out a strategy for growing his network in the fragmented world of social media. Not easy, since young viewers hop from smartphones, to YouTube, to cable, and to a dizzying array of other options as they follow their favorite programs. TV watching is no longer solely "linear"—it is increasingly "digital." Selling ads in the digital world is a big problem, because ratings agencies have difficulty tracking the actual number of people who watch a show. For that reason, pricing ads is tricky. Alterman needs to think differently about his business. As one of his fellow executives put it, "One of the things we've been trying to do over the last few years is not think of ourselves as a TV network anymore—we're a brand."

In our terms, Alterman and his team have defined an important value: they aspire to transform the network into a brand. The question is how to do it. Answer: they experiment.

At any given time, Comedy Central is running multiple experiments. Louis C.K. and Jerry Seinfeld experiment in small clubs. In a business, experimentation takes different forms, which sometimes generate money as well as insights. During a recent month, Alterman and his team were considering 73 different series and one-off specials in various stages of development. Ideas are produced through the pitching process. Young talents are invited to the Comedy Central offices to make pitches, and pitch again if the first one fails to hit the mark. Pilot shows and specials that are produced offer an opportunity to develop content and talent at the same time. The comic Amy Schumer got her break when she delivered a monologue at a Charlie Sheen roast. That performance led to several offers, but it also helped spread the word about her sketch series that was still two years away from airing.

A few comics receive "umbrella deals," which provide more opportunities for experimentation. Umbrella deals cover various aspects of a performer's material, in exchange for exclusive rights to any work that appears on television. A young artist named Hannibal Buress recently negotiated a deal that included a stand-up special, a pilot, and a role in a series. The pilot was "Unemployable" and involved Buress doing odd jobs like working on a goat farm. Alterman and his team felt the concept was flawed, but they liked the spirit of the show. It morphed into "Why? With Hannibal Buress." Buress comments: "The idea now is that I'll tackle different subjects with monologues, man-on-the-street interviews, sketches. So I can do some of the field stuff we were going to do on 'Unemployable,' but we're not constricted—we have more flexibility."

By television industry standards, Alterman's team has a relatively small development budget—between $250 million and

$350 million—but it produces outsized results. A big reason is the multifaceted, flexible experimentation process. Alterman explains: "Doing a half-dozen episodes [for the web is] significantly cheaper than doing a traditional, standalone pilot, and in a way we [get] more out of it. [Performers get to] evolve the characters, which they couldn't have done in a one-off episode." According to Jason Nadler, another Comedy Central producer: "The idea that you can get a better sense of how something works with a 22-minute pilot that you're focus-group testing at a Vegas casino, versus putting it online and seeing an actually engaged audience respond to it, is ridiculous."

> **Innovation Kick-Starter: Tinker**
> How can we create work-based experiments to test and refine our ideas?

Respect Tradition

In his insightful memoir *Life*, Rolling Stone Keith Richards[17] writes movingly about the roots of his creativity: "What I found about the blues and music, tracing things back, was nothing came from itself. As great as it is, this is not one stroke of genius. This cat was listening to somebody and it's his variation on the theme. And so you suddenly realize that everybody's connected here. This is not just that he's fantastic and the rest are crap; they're all interconnected." In other words, all innovation is basically variations on a theme that some creative person has already produced.

Like many innovators, Richards understands the importance of being a student of your field. So does Apple's chief designer Jonathan Ive. Apple's signature products like the iPod and the iPhone have historical roots that go back decades. The iPod owes a debt to the 1958 Braun T3 radio,[18] while the iPhone can trace its

lineage to an IBM/Bell South smartphone that had only two buttons: one for on/off and one for volume.

We think creative artists and designers like Richards and Ive intuitively understand the "limited scope principle." In their book *Creative Cognition: Theory, Research, and Applications,* Ronald Finke, Thomas Ward, and Steven Smith show that limiting the number of variables you consider actually leads to innovation. The explanation is that limits promote focus, which stimulates creativity.

> *Innovation Kick-Starter: Respect Traditon*
> How can we educate ourselves about the traditions relevant to our work?

You might be thinking that this finding contradicts what we said earlier about multiplying perspectives. But actually it does not. Innovation requires *both* broadening and narrowing your thinking. Both profusion—even *con*fusion—and analysis. Both multiplication and filtering.

Create a "Third Place"

Starbucks founder Howard Schultz took a trip to Italy when he was a young man.[19] He had an insight there that launched his world-changing business: for Europeans, along with the workplace and the home, a café is a "third place," as he puts it. They go to that third place to relax, socialize, and learn. Schultz came home from that trip with the desire to create such a place for Americans.

As much as possible, your team meetings should have the feeling of that third place, because it is in such a place that innovation happens. Research done by psychologist Kevin Dunbar vividly illustrates this point.[20] Dunbar wanted to understand scientific inspiration and felt that interviews produced a misleading conception of it. In an interview, everyone tends to simplify past experiences, producing neat hyper-rational narratives that leave out all the messiness that characterizes life as we live it. So Dunbar set up cameras at four leading laboratories and filmed as much of the activity as possible. All of the recorded interactions were transcribed and coded, using categories such as "clarification" and "questioning." The surprising finding is that most new ideas emerged during lab meetings, when researchers would informally present their work to colleagues. Conversation turns out to be one of the most important innovation tools.

Jay Leno had a "third place" insight that changed his entire career.[21] His act used to include a lot of traditionally structured jokes—with a beginning, middle, and punch line. Then one day, over lunch with a group of comedian friends, he told a story about something that happened to him on the road. The story lacked a classic joke structure, but his friends were laughing. Leno remembers thinking: "*Gee, they're laughing harder with this than with anything else in my act.*" The next night, on stage, he started with that story. The audience laughed as hard as his friends did. Leno said to himself: "*Ooh, here is a major breakthrough for me.*" Many comedians tell similar stories about having career-altering insights while having conversations over a meal with other comedians.

Innovation happens in that "third place," where intense, focused conversations ignite the passion that propels creativity. Psychologist R. Keith Sawyer was a jazz musician[22] before he became a professor at Washington University, and now he studies the "flow state" that promotes the creativity so often displayed by great athletes and improvisational artists. His findings suggest that innovation happens *between* people, not "inside [anyone's] head."

He elaborates: "What makes for a great creative team? Whether it's musicians, improv acts, or business teams, there are three elements to creative teams: trust, familiarity of members with one another, and a shared commitment to the same goals. These can enhance the performance of any group."

> **Innovation Kick-Starter: Create a "Third Place"**
> How can we create a "third place" environment in our meetings?

Innovation takes discipline. It is too easy to recycle the same old ideas your team has always been working on. One of the most effective ways to stimulate new thinking is to engage passionately with other people. Innovation is a social process. In the next chapter, we show how leadership at its best is also social.

Innovation Pain Point
Closing the Gap. Teams that say they want to be innovative often struggle because they fixate on a small number of ideas.
Teamwork Tip
Create a "third place" atmosphere in your meetings.
3x3 Spotlight
To boost innovation:
1. Define values in your chartering discussion.
2. Multiply perspectives and tinker.

8 Lead or Follow? Guidelines for Leadership Groups

It was the best of decisions, it was the worst of decisions, it was the epitome of wisdom, it was the height of foolishness—in short, the team demonstrated its considerable strengths and exposed its shocking limitations.

The executive team at Ford Motor Company in the 1950s played a leading role in a tale of two decisions that produced dramatic outcomes at the corporation. One decision involved saving the storied V-8 engine—a motor with nearly enough full-bore power to set a land speed record and unquestionably enough consumer appeal to sell millions of cars. The other led to the development and manufacture of a disastrous product: the Edsel, a name that has become synonymous with an utter lack of market focus. One striking aspect of this tale is that largely the same group of leaders made both decisions.

This chapter is about the lessons to be learned from this and other tales of leadership groups:

- Why does the very same leadership group make spectacularly good and spectacularly bad decisions?
- How can your leadership group avoid making those spectacularly bad decisions?

- How can your leadership group use social networks to multiply the power of formal authority?

An Automotive Love Affair

Chase Morsey Jr. almost single-handedly saved the V-8,[1] as he tells the reader in his aptly titled autobiography, *The Man Who Saved the V-8*. Someone who has the capacity to credit himself with that tremendous feat will also make no bones about driving "one of the most important product decisions in the history of Ford Motor Company." Morsey had good reasons to be proud of his accomplishment, but he also owed at least part of his success to the impressive flexibility shown by Ford's top executives. They were willing to listen to him and reverse a decision that had broad, public support from senior management across the company.

Morsey loved the V-8 with a passion that imbued his conversations and presentations at Ford with religious zeal. The love affair started when he was a teenager in the 1930s. Not long after his sixteenth birthday, Morsey returned home one afternoon from the Country Day School, a prestigious St. Louis college preparatory academy, to find an unexpected present waiting for him in the driveway: a new Ford coupe. He put literally thousands of miles on the car driving around town and then took it with him to Amherst College, where as circulation manager for the school paper he demonstrated the sales prowess that would propel him through an extraordinary business career. On trips back and forth from Massachusetts to Missouri, he would beam as gas station attendants expressed their awe of his beautiful machine:

"I see you got one of those Ford V-8s," an attendant would observe.

"Yep!" Morsey would answer.

"Wow! You've got the best!" was the typical comeback, which Morsey never tired of hearing.

After graduation, Morsey passed on a likely spot at the Harvard Law School to work for IBM. His father thought Morsey would learn skills there that would keep him out of the trenches in the war that the United States was about to enter. His father turned out to be right: Morsey eventually landed in an Air Force unit called Statistical Control and spent World War II overseeing the IBM operation at an Ohio base called Wright Field.

Morsey learned something else at IBM that served him well at Ford, after the war. He developed an appreciation for the customer. "My secret was taking prospective clients to our customers' businesses so that they could see how our customers were using our machines. I made those existing customers my assistant salesmen." He leveraged his customers in the same way, years later, when he put his job on the line and argued before the Ford executive team that the company should save the V-8.

In 1948, Morsey joined Ford as a budget analyst and soon took responsibility for the product planning department. One of the first documents he reviewed as department head was called "The Forward Plan for the Ford Car." He was thrilled to be part of a team shaping the company's future—until he realized that the V-8 had no place in it. The Forward Plan was built around the V-6. Many of the company's top executives had spent years at General Motors and were recruited because of their track record in growing the rival's business. GM's highly successful Chevrolet did not offer a V-8 as an option, and they saw no reason why the Ford car should either. Also, Ford was losing money and needed to cut costs, so the fact that the "bean counters" (in Morsey's words) claimed the V-8 was more expensive to manufacture than the alternative V-6 offered another reason to end the relationship with Morsey's great love.

But Morsey would have none of it. He believed the success of the Ford car depended on keeping the V-8: "I know that a Chevrolet could get me from my home to work just as well as any Ford, but that big V-8 under the hood kept me from ever thinking about switching brands. For me, buying a car was different from buying a toaster. It was a deeply emotional and personal experience." But he backed up his emotions with three months of market research and financial analysis. By the time he stepped into the intimidating Ford boardroom—"a round chamber dominated by a large, horseshoe-shaped table fashioned out of rich blond wood"—and saw Henry Ford II sitting shoulder to shoulder with the officers of the company, Morsey was ready to make his case.

He stood directly before Henry Ford's grandson and began: "For the past three months, I and my team have been talking to dealers and to customers, asking what they think about the decision to do away with the V-8. Ninety percent of consumers told us that they would be willing to pay up to $100 more for a car equipped with one than they would for the same automobile equipped with a six-cylinder motor." He had the team's attention and then he delivered a near-knockout punch: "By employing the latest manufacturing techniques, we can reduce the cost differential between a V-8 and a six to just $16."

Ford's executive vice-president Ernest Breech, a trained accountant known for raising tough issues, pressed Morsey hard for several minutes. Morsey had an answer for Breech's every question and countered all of his objections. Finally, Morsey exclaimed: "The V-8 engine *is* the Ford car. It is also the *only* advantage we have over Chevrolet."

Breech stared. Morsey stared. Time passed. Breech said: "I vote that we keep the V-8 engine." After further discussion, so did the rest of the executive team.

The upshot? Morsey later observed: "Armed with its new V-8 engine, Ford almost managed to catch up with Chevrolet in 1954. Ford was back."

Team, Know Thyself

Let's leave the Ford Motor Company of the 1950s for the moment and consider what we can learn about high performance teamwork from this meeting about the V-8.

V-8 Lesson 1: Slow Is Often Better than Fast In terms popularized by decision-theorist Daniel Kahneman[2] in his book *Thinking Fast* *and Slow,* Breech and his colleagues engaged "System 2" (or "slow") thinking—careful, deliberate reflection—and disciplined the natural impulse to let more automatic "System 1" (or automatic, "fast") processes drive the discussion to a foregone conclusion. This feat was  even more impressive in that the team had *already committed* to kill the V-8. It would have been easy to let the well-documented confirmation bias lead them to discount evidence that their very public commitment should be reversed. The confirmation bias leads you to look for facts that confirm decisions you want to make and undervalue facts that buttress an opposing perspective.

V-8 Lesson 2: Beware of Groupthink

The Ford team also demonstrated an impressive ability to avoid groupthink. A powerful and destructive form of social pressure, groupthink makes ideas nearly impervious to criticism. If you notice that one or two people who have opposing viewpoints are unfairly discounted or discredited by the rest of your team, there is a good chance that groupthink holds sway. Many of the executives who heard Morsey make his impassioned plea for the V-8 had worked together for years at GM, yet they resisted the common tendency to think like the people one works with. Not only did Morsey urge the executives to reverse a decision they had recently made, he was also asking them to overcome the natural cultural bias they had developed as GM executives. GM was the industry leader, and they had helped establish it in that position. At GM, they had deemphasized the V-8. Why not do the same at Ford? But at that fateful meeting in the Ford boardroom, they gave their support to Morsey.

How Easy It Is to Forget: The $250 Million Mistake

Meanwhile, back at the Ford Motor Company of the 1950s, the executive team was mulling another decision.

This one took shape right in the middle of the decade:[3] 1955, which legendary *New Yorker* journalist John Brooks describes as The Year of the Automobile. Near the end of the previous year, the company's forward product planning committee issued a report that predicted the U.S. gross domestic product would grow by $135 billion to $535 billion in a decade. Other trends were even more suggestive, from the vantage point of Ford's investment priorities. More than half of all families would generate annual incomes of $5,000, and a significant percentage of the extra cash would be devoted to automotive purchases. As a result, the number of cars on the road would grow from 50 million to 70 million. Close to half of those cars would be in the medium-price range. Bottom line: the executive team would be remiss if it failed to capitalize on these eye-popping numbers.

Another emerging pattern lent urgency to this idea. As incomes grew, consumers tended to "trade up." Some of them bought the medium-priced Ford Mercury, but more of them opted for similarly positioned GM brands: Oldsmobile, Buick, and Pontiac. Lewis Crusoe, vice president of the Ford Motor Company, complained, "We have been growing customers for General Motors." The company needed to create another medium-priced make that would capture the imagination—and harness the burgeoning purchasing power—of the expanding middle class.

Enter the Edsel, which was originally called, during the development phase leading up to its rollout, the "E-car"—"E" for "experimental." The car's lead designer, Roy A. Brown, had a clear goal. In his words, he wanted "to create a vehicle which would be unique in the sense that it would be readily recognizable in styling theme from the 19 other makes of cars on the road at the time." Fairfax M. Cone, head of the agency that managed the Edsel's advertising campaign, described this readily recognizable vehicle as "the smart car for the middle-income or professional family on its way up." It had a highly unusual vertical radiator grille that some thought looked like a horse-collar, and in the rear it sported wide horizontal wings, when most cars of the day were fitted with vertical ones. Drivers on the way up would be noticed tooling around town with their families in this standout vehicle.

The reception that the design initially received from senior leaders suggested one of two possibilities: a spectacular success was in the offing, or decision-makers were fooling themselves. Picture this scene: Executives were gathered at Ford's styling center, where an E-car prototype was parked behind a curtain. For nearly a minute after the curtain was lifted, the audience sat silent, as though stunned. Then Breech started clapping. Seconds later, wild applause erupted. The crowd had expressed its enthusiastic approval.

We all know how this story turns out. Consumers greeted the Edsel with decidedly less enthusiasm than the Ford executives who had their first glimpse of it at the styling center. In the end, Ford is estimated to have lost $250 million—over $2 billion in today's dollars—on the Edsel debacle. What makes the whole affair so compelling is the atmosphere of mania that enveloped nearly every part of it. Consider just a few of the most outlandish details, incredible if they were not fully documented:

- *The Poetry of Naming*. The company commissioned several research firms to conduct market research about a name for what was then still called the "E-car." When the firms produced inconclusive results, an internal group facilitated its own naming sessions with a similarly disappointing output. It was then that a marketing director named David Wallace prevailed upon the poet Marianne Moore to weigh in. She proposed such outré choices as Utopian Turtletop and Mongoose Civique. Ford planners decided Moore's names would never do, and they turned to Fairfax Cone for help. His firm organized a naming contest among its employees who generated 18,000 names and then, sensing less might be more, narrowed that number down to 6,000. An assistant general manager at Ford pushed back and the agency boiled down the remaining thousands to 10. When the names were presented to

Ford's executive committee, Breech declared, "I don't like any of them." Breech asked to see other names that had been rejected in earlier discussions. One of the candidates was the name of Henry Ford's only son—Edsel—an option that Edsel's own sons had said Edsel would probably have objected to. "Let's call it that," said Breech, and the matter was settled.

- *Expensive Hoopla*. Ford organized several expensive launch events. After one of them, journalists were allowed to drive home in Edsels in order to deliver them to local showrooms. One Edsel lost its oil pan and broke down in a town called Paradise, Kansas. Another crashed into a tollgate when the brakes failed. One driver just exercised poor judgment and totaled his car in some unnamed spot. Bad news continued to dog the rollout. Weeks after the Edsel arrived in showrooms around the country, Ford bankrolled a television special for the ill-fated auto that starred Bing Crosby and Frank Sinatra. The $400,000 spent on the extravaganza failed to move sales.

In 1960, the Edsel was effectively phased out. Only 2,846 cars were produced that year. In total, from launch to discontinuation, 109,810 were sold, and the company lost approximately $3,200 on each one. As John Brooks observed, Ford would have been better off just giving away the same number of Mercurys.

What Can the Edsel Debacle Teach Us?

Let's ask one more time what can be learned from this tale of two decisions. From the short, sorry history of the Edsel, we can draw two additional lessons:

Edsel Lesson 1: Good Teams Made Bad Mistakes By "good," we mean "composed of reasonable, competent people." Of course, it should come as no surprise that good teams make mistakes, since we saw in Part One that groups of high-IQ individuals often underperform, if not in so public a manner as the Ford executives did. But the twist in this case is that Breech and his colleagues performed in a way that turned their decision-making in the V-8 deliberation on its head. When Morsey presented his case in the

boardroom, the executives were willing open their minds and give him a fair hearing. This notable fact implies the second lesson.

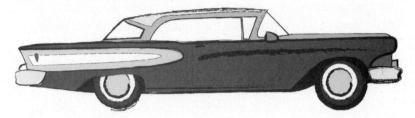

Edsel Lesson 2: Top Teams That Have Performed Well in the Past Are Often Derailed by Common Biases   In managing the development and launch of the Edsel, Breech and the other executives displayed the very biases they avoided so impressively in their encounter with Morsey. Take groupthink, for example. First-hand accounts suggest it took hold in that initial burst of applause and choked off productive discussions for years afterward. The team also made the mistake of being too deferential to their leader. When Breech unilaterally announced that henceforth the E-Car would be known as the Edsel, he short-circuited a team decision-making process. In other words, the decision was really just *his* decision—the leader's—and not the team's. Over time, constrained by a whole catalogue of biases, the team's thinking became increasingly insular, and it produced a consumer product that had precious little consumer appeal. Quotes from Ford managers during this period show how badly they had lost touch with the market. In 1960, looking back on the development of the Edsel, David Wallace reflected: "There's some irrational factor in people that makes them want one kind of car rather than another—something that has nothing to do with the mechanism at all, but with the car's personality, as the customer imagines it." But Wallace was wrong about that irrational factor. In fact, it made the *executives* want a car that few customers imagined or actually wanted.

Back to Basics: Keeping Your Top Team on Track

Our tale of two decisions shows that top teams never overcome the need to focus on the fundamentals of high-performance collaboration.

While there is no guarantee that your top team will always make V-8-type decisions and avoid disasters like the Edsel, we have identified three questions that will help you stay on track. We recommend devoting at least part of a team meeting once a month to reviewing these essential questions.

Are We Still Having Productive Discussions?

Like the executives who ran Ford Motor Company in the 1950s, top teams produce mixed results. One reason is the predictable entropy that afflicts leadership groups. According to one study, less than 10 percent of top teams were prepared to make good decisions,[4] and approximately a fifth of the teams were dominated by CEOs who made unilateral decisions. Even if norms were established in the first place, the findings indicate that most executive teams need to review how they make and communicate decisions. Not surprisingly, the need may be greatest when senior executives from different organizations are teaming up after a merger or acquisition (M&A). Research shows that only a third of for-profit companies deliver meaningful value for shareholders post-M&A and that the leading reason for poor returns has to do with underperforming top teams.

Reviewing norms has a positive impact not only on executive team members but also on their entire organization. The research done by management professor Anneloes Raes reveals that effectiveness cascades down from the top. [5] Employees at companies with high-functioning leadership teams exhibit more energy, more cognitive capacity, and more willingness to collaborate. Conversely, workplace expert Christine Porath[6] has found that poor leaders make it less likely that others share ideas, process information, ask for help when they need it, and deliver satisfying customer service.

Given these synergistic effects, both positive and negative, it pays to assess the strength of your agreement or disagreement by responding to a few simple statements regarding your top team's interactions. To make this easy, we suggest your team take a brief survey that has been shown to reveal key characteristics that help or hinder group effectiveness (see Figure 8.1).

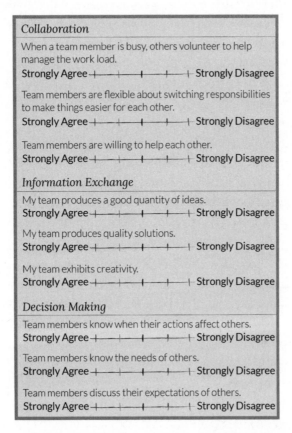

Collaboration

When a team member is busy, others volunteer to help manage the work load.
Strongly Agree ⊢—⊢—⊢—⊢—⊣ Strongly Disagree

Team members are flexible about switching responsibilities to make things easier for each other.
Strongly Agree ⊢—⊢—⊢—⊢—⊣ Strongly Disagree

Team members are willing to help each other.
Strongly Agree ⊢—⊢—⊢—⊢—⊣ Strongly Disagree

Information Exchange

My team produces a good quantity of ideas.
Strongly Agree ⊢—⊢—⊢—⊢—⊣ Strongly Disagree

My team produces quality solutions.
Strongly Agree ⊢—⊢—⊢—⊢—⊣ Strongly Disagree

My team exhibits creativity.
Strongly Agree ⊢—⊢—⊢—⊢—⊣ Strongly Disagree

Decision Making

Team members know when their actions affect others.
Strongly Agree ⊢—⊢—⊢—⊢—⊣ Strongly Disagree

Team members know the needs of others.
Strongly Agree ⊢—⊢—⊢—⊢—⊣ Strongly Disagree

Team members discuss their expectations of others.
Strongly Agree ⊢—⊢—⊢—⊢—⊣ Strongly Disagree

Figure 8.1 Top Team Development Survey adapted from Raes[7]

If your answers fall more to the right side of the scales, then you should ask whether your team is really just a co-acting group or even one that sends results-impeding ripples across your organization. A reasonable next step would be to consider spending a full meeting on norms, following the chartering process we detailed in Chapter 1. As we have said, high-performing teams are always revisiting their commitments, in an iterative process that is never complete.

Another closely related question you should consider is whether there is enough followership on your team. In a now-classic article in the *Harvard Business Review*,[8] leadership expert Robert E. Kelly makes a case for developing followers. Just as some CEOs display subpar leadership skills, some team members are ineffective followers. We saw how important followership was in saving the V-8. Morsey could have simply implemented "The Forward Plan for the Ford Car." Instead, he pushed back on the top team in a respectful, credible way, displaying the defining characteristics of a good follower. Kelly maintains that organizations should develop followers the way they develop leaders, offering training in self-management, critical thinking, persuasion, and the ability to alternate between leading and following. We suggest you also put a discussion of followership on your monthly agenda, using answers to the survey to prompt reflection on the behaviors your team thinks exemplify this important concept.

A review of your norms might raise some difficult issues, but it will ultimately recharge your performance. Over time, perceptions of effectiveness diverge and can be a source of discord. In a surprising number of cases, leaders have a much more positive perspective on their team's performance than other members do. One study shows that roughly a third of CEOs[9] believe their teams could do better at fostering innovation and building a culture, while over half of the other team members see an opportunity for improvement. A related survey of HR executives[10] reveals that only 6 percent of them believe "the executives in our C-suite are a well-integrated team." These findings suggest that revisiting norms can lead to some uncomfortable conversations. But it will also produce better decisions—decisions that have been considered from multiple angles and are informed by input from colleagues with divergent opinions.

Good teams that neglect these fundamentals make mistakes, as the Edsel story illustrated. In case you think such an adventure could happen only in the benighted 1950s, just recall the equally disastrous results when Roberto Guizueta[11] made the virtually unilateral decision to introduce New Coke in the 1980s, replacing the classic formula for a drink that consumers had come to worship. Announcing the rollout at a glitzy New York press conference, he declared, "The best just got better." Less than three months later, New Coke had disappeared from the market. It took Ford somewhat longer to reverse course, at much greater expense.

Do we need to realign our priorities?

MIT researchers have shown that high-level agreements about goals[12] can mask deeper misalignments that affect top team performance. These misalignments reflect naturally evolving differences over the relative importance of issues such as profit, corporate responsibility, and customer satisfaction. When these differences go unaddressed, teams are slower to make decisions and implement them—or, often a worse outcome, implement them in the wrong way. During her tenure as Xerox CEO, Anne Mulcahy made a point of encouraging top team members to publicly discuss conflicting perceptions and interpretations of stated goals. The open exchange promoted engagement. As Mulcahy observed, leaders who "consider a diverse set of opinions ... create 'followership' around decisions that might not come naturally."

You should also periodically revisit even the most basic priorities, like a corporate commitment to following relevant laws or regulations. The scandalous story of how GE executives ran afoul of U.S. antitrust statutes[13] in the late 1950s demonstrates how easily colleagues fall out of sync, even without being aware of misinterpreting one another and acting on contradictory assumptions about goals. In testimony before Congress, William S. Ginn, a GE sales executive, recounts a conversation with his direct superior, Robert Paxton, about a company rule called Directive Policy 20.5: "No employee shall enter into any understanding, agreement, plan or scheme, expressed or implied, formal or informal, with any competitor, in regard to prices, terms or conditions of sale, production, distribution, territories, or customers; nor exchange or discuss with a competitor prices, terms or conditions of sale, or any other competitive information."

The law was the law. Although there was no need to enshrine it in corporate policy, GE's leadership wanted to leave no doubt. Nonetheless, highly paid sales executives like Ginn simply did not believe that 20.5 was anything more than a fig leaf and questioned Paxton on whether he really believed it needed to be followed. But Paxton was unequivocal about his executive team's intentions: "We mean it, and these are your orders." The problem was that, after hearing Paxton's forceful statement, Ginn had meetings with other executives, who intentionally or not raised questions about the commitment to 20.5. The result: Ginn went to town on price fixing. When investigators pressed him about it, Ginn said, "The people who were advocating the Devil were able to sell me better than the philosophers that were selling the Lord."

Not long after the conversation with Paxton, Ginn was promoted and he converted to the 20.5 religion. But Ginn's attempts to keep his flock from straying were just as ineffectual as Paxton's. While Ginn sermonized, his people aggressively pursued their sinful price-fixing ways around the country, even after signing their names to the 20.5 document. Ginn ruefully commented: "I didn't sell this thing to the boys well enough . . . . A complete philosophy, a complete understanding, a complete breakdown of barriers between people [is needed] if we are going to get some understanding and really live and manage these companies within the philosophies that they should be managed in."

Lest you think Ginn is merely being self-serving in propounding his "philosophy" of communication, consider the testimony of Paxton, who was never accused of price-fixing: "Now, [a sales executive] could say, 'I told my boss what I was doing,' and his boss wouldn't have the foggiest idea what was being told to him, and both men could testify under oath, *one saying yes and the other saying no, and both be telling the truth*" (italics added). The point is that people who work together every day can over time become so misaligned in their thinking that the most vigorous efforts to communicate can produce exactly the opposite of the intended outcomes. Such is the power of misalignments—regarding values, assumptions, and styles—to cause the worst kinds of performance problems.

Comments made at the time by GE chairman Ralph J. Cordiner were the most surprising of all. Cordiner was a well-known evangelist of absolutely unfettered free enterprise and had made many proclamations about the importance of Directive 20.5. When he learned that his explicit commands to respect it had been ignored, he expressed "great alarm" and "great wonderment." This is yet another example of the well-documented problem that dogs every top team, at every level of an organization: team members fall out of sync, just as married couples do. You think you are clearly communicating your intentions, but really you are speaking to yourself about the assumptions you are making about what you believe others are hearing. A well-known *New Yorker* cartoon captured this dynamic in an exchange between an exasperated husband and his distraught wife. The husband faces the wife, who is looking away, and says: "Of course I care about how you imagined I thought you perceived I wanted you to feel."

We will let the playwright George Bernard Shaw have the final—slightly updated—say on the challenge of aligning your team behind a set of goals: "The single biggest problem in communicating your goals is the illusion that others understand you."

Have We become Too Isolated?

Just as members of a top team need to make sure they are aligned behind shared priorities, the whole top team should ask whether it is aligned and connected enough with the rest of the organization and the broader environment. In this sense, every member of the team should make organizational relationship-building a priority.

Top teams are sometimes too concerned with their own discussions and lose sight of the need to relate to others. As one executive at an investment bank put it:[14] "If I consider what our top team needs to do, [I would say we need] to have different networks that execute quickly on crises or opportunities—combining our expertise and that of other groups in the company. Building this ability to solve big problems quickly is a big deal, because the pace of business keeps ramping up. Yet we don't focus enough on this, in contrast to internal team building and individual coaching." Studies reveal why these relationship networks are essential: 90 percent of the information a top team uses to make decisions comes through informal channels rather than formal reports.

A study of a global health sciences concern found that the entire membership of a high-performing top team—14 people—represented just 2 percent of the senior executives, yet accounted for 15 percent of all collaborative connections in the organization. This helps explain how top team alignment can produce ripple effects that have far-reaching positive or negative impacts on middle management and employees. The data also shows that a strong top team is often positioned at a hub of subgroups. Top team executives therefore have a dual alignment responsibility—one relates to their teammates, and the other to people and groups below them on the org chart and even outside their organization.

When Michael Bloomberg was mayor of New York City,[15] he broke down the barriers between his top team and the rest of his organization by creating a "bullpen." Bloomberg sat in the middle of a small, often busy room where everyone could see and hear everyone else. As someone who worked in the bullpen put it: "As a workspace, it is something that you do not think that you can ever get used to. . . . But when you see the mayor hosting high level meetings in clear sight of everyone else, you start to understand that this open communication model is not bullshit." Organizational experts Robert I. Sutton and Huggy Rao[16] have observed that leaders who actively make connections with people across an organization work as hard as someone in a "high-maintenance personal relationship." Although the bullpen had its challenges as a work environment, Bloomberg designed it so that leaders had to pay attention to this kind of relationship maintenance every day.

Multiplier Top Teams

Best-selling authors Liz Wiseman and Greg McKeown say that the best leaders make everyone smarter,[17] describing them as "multipliers." Multipliers work through others, inspiring their passion and commitment. Multipliers neutralize the negative effects of social loafing and engage the full potential of teammates and co-workers.

We think the "multiplier" label can be applied to the best top teams, who create the optimal conditions for decision-making, align the functions of an organization, and build relationship networks that facilitate speedy information flow and implementation. Multiplier top teams are careful to avoid the leadership mistakes that led to high profile fiascos at Ford Motor Company and Coca-Cola. In an era of "new demands and insufficient resources," as David Allen has observed,[17] organizations face problems that can only be solved by a high-performing team and a team of teams.

Sue Siegel confronted such a problem when she was president of Affymetrix, a producer of microarray technologies used in analyzing genetic material. Affymetrix had been growing smartly for three years after going public, when Siegel learned that a key device was liable to report inaccurate results in a small number of tests. Should the company issue a product recall? Siegel was an experienced executive in the life sciences industry and knew the technology cold. Many executives would have closed ranks and made the decision with a small number of trusted advisers or even by themselves. But Siegel was a multiplier. She organized a forum that included employees and managers from across the company and facilitated a large-group discussion that examined the potential impact of a recall on customers, financial performance, and legal obligations. Siegel also acted as a decision architect in that she designed the review process to ensure that she and her top team received broad input from across the company.

After several rounds of debate, the top team convened to review what it had heard at the forum. The eventual decision to recall the product took a serious bite out of Affymetrix's market cap. But two quarters later, the company was as strong as ever, because employees were able to explain the recall to customers and use the setback as an occasion to deepen relationships with them. For fours years afterward, with Siegel and her multiplier team at the top, Affymetrix consistently exceeded revenue and earnings expectations.

Multiplier top teams are HPTs, working hard to develop productive working relationships that facilitate communication and support high-quality decision processes aligned with shared priorities. This chapter showed how asking the right questions can help keep your top team on track and multiply the impact of your organization's people and assets. In the next chapter, we examine how to build effective and productive committees.

Top Teams Pain Point

Isolation. Top teams tend to insulate themselves from the operational and customer-facing realities of their organizations. They also have trouble seeing beyond their own opinions.

Teamwork Tip

Periodically assess decision-making processes and leverage social networks.

3x3 Spotlight

To keep your team connected to the broader organization:

1. Commit to share information with people outside the team.

2. Actively incorporate outside perspectives and data into your decision-making.

9 Why Are We Here? Engaging Committees

T he chair of the search committee enters the conference room carrying a small, black, cardboard box. As though it were a sacred relic, he places it carefully on the table and steps back, gazing in turn at each member of the committee.

"What's with the box?" we ask ourselves. Aside from the chair, everyone seems as confused as we are.

The chair brings everyone to attention. "Let us begin," he intones, like a clergyman. "We are going to have a vote." He opens the box and pulls out a stack of note cards. He prepares to distribute them. Over the years, in leading the nonprofit board, he has developed a well-deserved reputation for meticulous planning, and he clearly knows what he wants to do this evening.

Slowly we begin to understand the situation. Then suddenly it all makes sense: the chair has decided to use a vote to conclude, once and for all, a painful, contentious search for a new executive director.

Our fellow committee members seem to have reached the same conclusion. Sitting to our left, Carol begins to raise her hand, which floats in mid-air. A managing partner at a major consulting firm, she is a nationally prominent expert on hiring processes. But at the moment she looks puzzled about *this* hiring process. "A *vote?* What vote?" she asks as her hand hovers over her papers.

"We have debated long enough. We need to move on. It is time to make a decision about a candidate," replies the chair.

"I thought we were going to make a decision by consensus," she protests. "We never discussed voting. I feel blind-sided." Others concur, expressing varying degrees of irritation and anger. But the chair

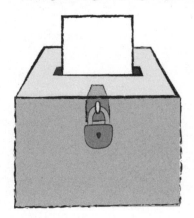

persists, imposing his will on the rest of the committee by force.

A vote is taken, and a decision is made. Strictly speaking, when the evening ended, the committee had done its job. It disbanded after this meeting. But the negative fallout lasted for months. The organization broke into warring camps. Board members resigned and donations plummeted.

3x3?

Like many committees, ours illustrated just about all of the ways teamwork can go wrong. Meetings were heavy on procedure but light on the kind of process that produces commitment and passion. Goals and responsibilities were unclear. Committee members had no opportunities to course-correct as the process unfolded. The whole effort kept lurching forward, like a steamroller.

Though our search committee was a study in dysfunction, many committees do valuable work. Making good decisions about hiring and strategy often requires input from a diverse group of organizational insiders and outsiders. But it is notoriously difficult to engage the right committee members in the right way. This chapter tells you how to do it.

To Committee, or Not to Committee—That Is the Question

The first question you should ask about your committee: Does it even need to exist?

Getting rid of just one committee can have nearly transformative effects. Exaggeration? Consider the results of a Bain and Company study.[1] It calculated the number of man-hours devoted to supporting one weekly executive committee meeting. The researchers used data-mining tools to analyze the Outlook calendars of everyone in the organization and tracked the committee's ripple effects. The committee members themselves spent 7,000 hours per year in meetings. But the whole organization was sucked into the vortex. The Bain group calculated the time members spent meeting with their unit chiefs to prepare for committee activities, and the time each chief spent meeting with their section heads ... and so on. In total, just one committee cost the company 300,000 hours per year. Keep this number in your head next time you think there is no harm in creating *just one more committee*.

At worst, a committee can become the automatic default for decision-making—a collective form of punting the ball down the field when in reality an effective decision could be made through other means. If a CEO or leader is concerned about backlash from acting unilaterally, creating a committee is an easy way to mitigate the risk of making the wrong decision. As committees proliferate to review every initiative in the organization, it can get to the point where so many exist that people begin to despair at ever getting a proposal approved.

So, first thing's first. In order to decide if a committee really is the most effective tool for your needs, ask yourself the following three questions:

1. Would the decisions made by this committee materially affect the performance and objectives of the organization?
2. Is there an existing standing committee whose purpose could serve this decision?
3. Does this decision actually require diverse opinions and input from across the organization, or can it be made unilaterally?

How many of the committees at your organization would pass these tests? A major mining company[2] used a similar set of criteria and cut down their number of standing committees from 40 to 10. "We used to have a 'Red Book' that listed all the committees. We burned it—literally—and started over," said one executive.

By meticulously cultivating an idea or proposal before a committee is formed to review it, you are already well ahead of the game. Your colleagues will appreciate the advance work and understand that the committee is not just a time-waster.

Inspiring Passion

Let's assume you have reviewed the questions and decided that you do, in fact, need to create a committee to solve a problem. Now you face the daunting task of getting your members on the same page as part of a team that can often feel disconnected from "real work."

That was the challenge faced by one of our clients—a private construction company we will call Eastbrook. Regional directors were called to serve on a committee tasked with creating solutions to a new and pressing issue: recruitment and retention. With an aging workforce, in an industry that lacks appeal to millennials, Eastbrook was faced with major brain drain. The top team realized they needed to troubleshoot the pipeline of talent among engineers and project managers. They were used to having employees stay with the company for 20 to 40 years, and were at a loss when they started shedding seasoned veterans just as they began having a hard time bringing in younger millennials.

This situation was mission critical. The Eastbrook CEO and senior VPs had made it their top priority. Figuring out how to mitigate these trends would be the difference between the success and failure of a company over a hundred years old. But you wouldn't have known it from the way the retention committee members were acting. They complained that it was taking away from the work of getting projects completed. They had deadlines and budgets that were always top of mind. In the middle of meetings, they would walk out to take phone calls. Why didn't they see how vital their input was?

In trying to uncover the source of their flagging energy, we formulated three possible diagnoses. These potential misalignments can sap the passion of any committee at any organization. Let's take a look at each problem.

Get the right people in the room

"I don't understand what these numbers mean," Andrea commented to her teammates.

"Me neither," Juan sighed. The team looked around the table, wondering how much they needed to sell this round to cover fixed costs.

When we first started running the team formation process of the EDP simulation, we gave very little guidance about it to participants. Our directions were simple: Find seven other people and start talking. We soon realized that team members picked others with whom they had maybe shared a plane or a cab to Wharton. Not surprisingly, a whole lot more care was needed. Those teams without any finance or accounting expertise floundered—they didn't have the right people in the room. Without the right skill sets on their teams for the two-week exercise, participants became disengaged, complaining about pressing obligations in their organizations and leaving the room to take calls.

Sound familiar? Once we realized the issue, we started requiring that EDP teams include at least one person with a finance background and one with accounting. Once they had the skills they needed in the room, the teams' engagement shot up, since they felt they could actually achieve their goals.

What is true for EDP teams is true for committees, where it is tough to hold team members accountable, and they can quickly disengage if they sense the group does not have the right people to accomplish its objectives. Since committee members are often forced or assigned to serve on committees, it is critical for leaders to evaluate carefully whom they are choosing to serve.

The key considerations for committees are what we call the 5xS factors: size, schedule, skills, social capital, and styles. They can be applied to any team formation, but are especially crucial in the planning phase of committee work.

Size Depending on the goals of the committee, size may vary, but typically smaller numbers—six or seven members—mitigate the social loafing effect. This size also provides enough diversity of opinion.

Schedule Think carefully about who actually has the time to commit to being an effective committee member: Are they in the middle of a product launch? Do their travel schedules make it difficult to schedule time with them? Do they already serve on four committees? Review whether you need to set limits on how many committees and what percentage of their time you should allow key people to devote to this type of teamwork.

Skills While the point of a committee is to bring together diverse opinions for a special issue, make sure everyone who is in the room has a specific point of view or level of expertise that will add to the deliberations. Diversity for diversity's sake will not improve the effectiveness of your boards and committees.

Social Capital Who is respected in your organization? Who has strong ties across functions and departments? Assembling a committee of people who have high social capital can lend credibility to the outcomes of the committee. Also, since their reputations precede them, they can help create a better working environment. If these committee members are respected across the organization, trust-building on the team will be easier right off the bat.

Styles We have already discussed the importance of styles more generally. In teams where you have to make choices about who participates, devote time to curating a mix of styles to ensure that you limit the number of overly dominant or passive individuals.

The 5xS Factors

Meanwhile, back at our Eastbrook retention committee, we had reviewed the 5S factors and concluded that the right group had been assembled. First of all, it was a reasonable size of seven. In addition, committee members had set aside ample time to work on the retention problem, and they each had developed an informed opinion about it based on their own experience. Since everyone was also a powerful influencer, the group had the collective leverage needed to implement any organizational recommendations. And, lastly, a mix of styles was represented.

Figure Out What's Important

But what if the biggest issue relates to the all-important "What's in it for me?" (WIIFM) question that we raised in Chapter 1?

As an example, consider our experience on the executive committee of a national professional organization. We had just joined it and were energized about leading a subteam focused on building local networks for members of the association. Our colleague Jessica felt the same enthusiasm.

"Okay, so right now we need to get three more member interviews done, reach out to other professional organizations with strong local networks, and start to synthesize this into a report," we said on a conference call.

"I can take the interviews if you'll reach out. Then we can figure out how best to split up the report," Jessica energetically chimed in. So far so good, but the third person on the line—call her Samantha—was suspiciously silent. We were concerned, but between our enthusiasm and Jessica's, we felt everything would get done.

Unfortunately—well, fortunately for her—Jessica got a new job offer and had to bow out of the subcommittee as she left the association. Another member was placed on the team who seemed equally disengaged. The tone of the check-in meetings changed completely. We needed Samantha to step up. And while she always answered in the affirmative when asked to do a task, we did not see that she was making progress.

"So ... how is it going with scheduling those last two interviews?" we asked, having spent 20 minutes updating Samantha and the new member during the first meeting after Jessica's departure.

"Oh, that? Oh yeah, it's coming along. Definitely going to get working on it," Samantha unenthusiastically responded. The conversations went this way for months.

Why the energy gap between Jessica and Samantha? Since Jessica was a young academic building her career, she had a strong personal interest in the alumni networks to match her enthusiasm for the organizational goal. She thought these alumni contacts would be important for the organization, but they were also networks she could tap into herself. Samantha, a well-established department chair at a major university, had little need for building her LinkedIn connections. Our team had made a common committee mistake: we failed to figure out Samantha's WIIFM, hoping passion for the collective goals themselves would build energy.

As with this committee, getting the right team is just one step. When it is easy for members to disengage and suffer few consequences, the WIIFM questions become even more important. If they feel their service is unlikely to be valuable for them, you may never get their full attention.

You can start by asking a simple question: "What do you want to learn by participating in this committee?"

Learning goals are powerful motivators. They focus members on developing personal skills and knowledge while contributing to the team. Learning can come from a more in-depth understanding of the business or different functions, or simply learning about the people they are working with.

Back to our Eastbrook committee again: we checked the WIIFM motivation of each team member, and it was clear that they had that question answered. As the committee gave them visibility with the top team, there was no doubt this would boost their careers. In interviews, they also clearly saw benefit in thinking about how to become more skilled recruiters and managers. If they were a good fit for the group and saw the potential for learning, was there something else we needed to pay attention to?

WIIFMO? The issue clicked when we slightly modified the WIIFM question to: What's In It For My Organization? It became clear to us that the Eastbrook managers could not see how the retention issue affected their company, and how exactly the output of the committee would address the problem. We took a step back. We asked the managers to think about what retention meant for Eastbrook and where they saw the impact in their day-to-day work. As it turned out, the most productive conversations about this came not in the daylong sessions but during the evenings at the hotel bar where managers traded war stories about their experience in the field.

One such evening, a committee member, Kevin, walked in looking upset from a call he had just taken. "Everything okay?" a colleague asked. "I just lost another one of my engineers to a competitor down in Virginia." Kevin responded. He recounted how the individual who left, one of his best, had felt uncertain about his career path with the company, and had accepted an offer from a competitor even though it came with only a minor raise. His reason was simply that he could see a future for himself working up their corporate ladder.

Around the table there were nods and mumbles of empathy, and one story after another illustrated the challenge. A young rising star leaving after a couple of years for a different industry. An older veteran poached away by a competitor. It was becoming clear how their committee could make a difference at Eastbrook and what the company could do differently. Motivation clicked into place.

In subsequent meetings, there was a palpable fervor. Committee members realized how much they needed to solve this problem in order to help their own regions, and each other's. They saw the connection between their committee and the retention policies of the larger organization. They had found not just the WIIFM but the WIIFMO. It wasn't simply that doing well on this committee was good for their career in terms of impressing their superiors. This issue directly affected their day-to-day ability to get work done. Committee members told us they were spending hours outside of our meetings brainstorming and researching an actionable solution to the problem.

In clarifying the WIIFMO for your committee, aim for a simple, unified purpose. Management scholars Ram Charan and Mike Useem[3] call this a "central idea." In their book *Boards That Lead,* they explain: "The central idea references why the company exists, whom it serves, how it should be nurtured, why it will flourish, how it will make money and manage risk, and where it must be going if it is to sustain a competitive presence and achieve its broader purpose. Boards need to be sure the central idea is clear and compelling and that every board member understands it."

Committees similarly need a central idea that guides their actions. In helping teams develop one, we like to use the image of the Eiffel Tower. No matter where in Paris you are, you can look up to the tower and reorient yourself to find your way. That is what a central idea needs to do—orient the committee or board such that every decision can be measured against whether it takes them toward or away from the Tower. If it gets everyone on the team excited, then it can enable you to create the unicorn of committees: a fully committed team.

That central idea needs to be not only highly visible and attractive, it needs to be specific. The Eastbrook team was tasked with figuring out a broad talent management issue. However, early on they realized this included recruitment, retention, succession planning, and training.

They narrowed their focus to retention, and from there got even more granular—looking specifically at employee engagement as a key lever. They figured out a central idea, and were able to effectively problem-solve around it. Committees should similarly restrain themselves. Just as the Eastbrook group was able to take a broad mission and narrow it down to one high impact lever to act upon, teams need to know they can't tackle every problem. They will be more effective and more engaged if they are driven toward one landmark on the horizon.

Decide on Roles

As consultants, we help many different kinds of organizations solve their problems. There is one thing we do not do: design logos.

When our consulting firm embarked on a rebranding process, we created a committee that included one of our consultants, a partner, a designer, and an outside adviser. It was meant to be a project with a quick turnaround, with oversight and feedback from the rest of the team. But early on we ran into obstacles. There was confusion about who was "running the show." The consultant thought she was managing all of the different parties because she was the junior employee that was connected to all the parts. The outside adviser thought she was supposed to take the lead to free up the consultant's time for her more pressing concerns. And neither the consultant nor the adviser realized that the partner wanted a much bigger voice in the process than he was being given. The designer just wanted to know whom he was supposed to communicate with.

The confusion around roles led to stress, miscommunication, disputes, and some level of disengagement throughout the committee. When we took a breath and had open communications around everyone's expectations for their involvement and decision-making authority, we were able to smoothly move the process along. Suddenly, everyone became excited again about the possibilities and ideas presented by the designer. Role clarity is especially important on committees, because accountability can often be lacking and authority is often uncorrelated to seniority. To conclude our consideration of committees, let's look at these issues of expectation-setting and authority in roles.

Leverage Expectation-Setting   When our colleague Elizabeth Briody[4] took over as president of the board of a senior community, she had high hopes for bringing change to the organization. As an anthropologist, she felt she had a good grasp of the internal cultural strengths and weaknesses and the changing marketplace conditions. Her plans for renovating the facility were built on a new orientation toward proactive philanthropic outreach. However, neither the executive director of the organization nor the past president shared Briody's reasonable perspective. They continued to believe that the traditonal reliance on resident fees would keep the community afloat over the long term despite the deteriorating state of the 50-year-old facility.

Not surprisingly, given strong resistance at the top, a virulent anti-development campaign soon began to emerge. The Past President pushed to eliminate a large portion of the development budget. The Executive Director quietly spread animosity among her key staff and drove the development director to resign, essentially making the fundraising strategy moot. The executive director also ignored board requests for basic communication about the organization's operations. Tension and conflict erupted at board meetings. Very little was accomplished.

How many committees like this one have you been on? You meet month after month, have circular discussions for hours, and walk away wondering why you had just spent your valuable time in yet another unproductive meeting where nothing is ever resolved and no decisions are made. You wonder whether it would make a difference at all if you simply failed to show up. At the senior community, these typical misgivings ultimately led to the resignation of two thirds of the board. Briody's assessment was that a divisive spirit had overtaken the team, energy for future initiatives had been sapped, and the hoped-for "culture of philanthropy" would never take hold.

Seeing an opportunity to learn from this difficult situation, Briody compared it with others in which she had tried to help boards and committees avoid similar headaches. She realized that, in every case, she could have built stronger relationships with malcontents early on. She also saw that a strategic planning process could have served to align the members of a fractious board around common goals. However, even these measures would probably not have been enough to overcome entrenched resistance at the senior community.

Briody's most basic takeaway from her self-assessment: Expectations with teeth are critical to success.

The executive director simply had no incentive to work with the board, because there were no tangible consequences if she refused to follow their guidance. Due to the difficulties in filling senior managerial positions for this type of organization, even those who decried the executive director's job performance were reluctant to fire her. She is still in that role today, even as the organization continues to lose residents and the facility deteriorates.

We are generally not big fans of wielding the stick of accountability. But on committees you do need to set clear expectations for participation and agree upon meaningful consequences for when it falls short. On boards and other volunteer-based groups where there are few if any disincentives for slacking, members can easily become listless or disengaged, creating a drag on collective efforts. To avoid this all-too-common problem, Briody created a Countering Resistance Model that challenges non-profits to focus first on key relationships before engaging in a new piece of work or launching a new initiative. Developing trust is a crucial aspect of this relationship development, but it also must be coupled with expectation-setting to make sure everyone pulls their own weight.

Uncouple Authority and Seniority Sometimes it is the junior person who needs to take charge.

Consider, for example, this typical scene. At a global advertising firm, the worldwide managing director leans intently across his desk. He is engrossed in conversation with an employee in her mid-20s. It might look like he is offering guidance on her performance and career opportunities in the industry. In fact, just the opposite: she is the one offering guidance. As his reverse mentor, she is helping him understand how to pep up his Twitter account and stay current on popular music trends. Both are critical goals in the fast-paced, topical world of advertising.

Reverse mentoring can be an important aspect of committee work. Alan Webber, the co-founder of Fast Company,[5] explains the concept: "It's a situation where the old fogies in an organization realize that by the time you're in your forties and fifties, you're not in touch with the future the same way as the young twentysomethings. They come with fresh eyes, open minds, and instant links to the technology of our future." Compared to more senior committee members, junior colleagues often have more distinctive perspectives and more scheduling flexibility, and they can also find opportunities to build important leadership skills by taking charge on key tasks. For these reasons, even on high-profile committees, junior colleagues frequently act as reverse mentors, exercising authority even though they lack seniority.

Of course, the reshuffling of authority and seniority can produce confusion and tension. Traditionally, authority is associated with formal titles, defined by a set of responsibilities, and tied to job descriptions. Not only that, but it is usually older colleagues who wield the most authority, augmented by those formal titles. In committees, these well-established expectations can be—and often should be—upended.

To manage such potentially challenging situations, we recommend establishing informal roles. Leadership scholars Green and Molenkamp[6] define informal roles such as the caretaker, coordinator, or antagonist who helps a team accomplish tasks and build relationships in ways that formal roles tend not to cover. Acknowledging and designating informal roles are helpful on committees, and on any kind of team. Caretakers make sure that conflicts are handled productively. Coordinators make sure everyone understands what is expected of them. Antagonists challenge a team when it falls into groupthink.

It is in this spirit that we recommend paying attention to and even assigning informal roles on committees. These roles are often overlooked or dismissed, yet they act as the necessary oil that keeps the wheels of group process running smoothly. In doing committee work, senior members acting as subordinates will be more engaged if they can find a way to take up an explicit informal role, and junior colleagues will be more successful in directing more experienced teammates.

The Committed Committee

Keeping the energy up on committees is rarely easy. How can you keep team members engaged when they are not required to participate and are likely to put their committee role at the bottom of a long list of priorities? The first step is making

Committees Pain Point
Engagement. Members have day jobs, making it difficult to fully commit to group tasks.
Teamwork Tip
Clarify the WIIFM and WIIFMO.
3x3 Spotlight
To foster engagement:
1. Use the 5xS Factors to get the right people in the room.
2. Answer the WIIFM and WIIFMO questions.
3. Set clear expectations around roles and responsibilities.

sure the committee really is necessary. Once that is settled, you should make sure the right people are involved. Pay special attention to keeping the purpose crystal clear for both the organization and each person on the team. Combine the stick of accountability with the carrot of learning goals and informal roles. Use the 3x3 Framework, and your committee will have answered that all-important question: "Why are we here, anyway?"

Conclusion: The Future Is Teams

T he old workplace is dead. Long live the new workplace!

Slow-moving, top-down bureaucracies are disappearing. Disruptive technologies have increased connectivity and the speed of communication. Work is becoming more flexible—and just plain faster. Organizational boundaries are blurring.

You can read about these changes every day in the business press. For example, *The Economist* recently proclaimed:[1] "It is time to start caring about sharing." This was just the latest in a string of stories about the arrival of the so-called sharing economy. The term captures an essential aspect of the startups that are replacing service providers like taxi cab companies and hotels. These traditional businesses have been dominated by organizations with generous numbers of full-time employees. But pioneers such as Uber and Airbnb are based on a different model, providing virtual platforms to connect thousands of private individuals who offer services independently and on their own time.

The New Regime

Does anyone have a real job in a real organization anymore? *CIO Insight* has said that "outsourcing is the new normal." *Inc.* has introduced the new "anywhere office" being created by the growth of the flexible workforce. So, you have been warned. You need to pay more attention to new ways of collaborating and teaming. If not, you might find yourself out of the loop and out of work.

Hype or reality? Let's look more closely at the trends.

Will Your World Be Blue, Green, or Orange?[2]

You should take this question seriously.

Based on a survey of 10,000 employees and 500 human resource professionals around the globe, consulting firm, Price Waterhouse Coopers (PWC), created three different scenarios that define how the workplace might evolve by the year 2022. So sit back and imagine: Which future will you inhabit?

In the Blue World, big business dominates. Corporations continue to consolidate and integrate, taking over a larger share of private sector activity. You work in a big multinational where you expect to be employed for decades, with a level of job security that you could not have imagined 10 years ago. While your employment is stable, your work is anything but. In return for this security, you are expected to shift tasks constantly and quickly move up a steep learning curve. You need to be able to develop new working relationships with people who have just joined your organization—through the hiring process or through acquisitions. You also have to stay in sync with colleagues in a network of firms your organization partners with on an ad hoc basis. Far from meaning more top-down management, you find that your company is happy to let you self-manage this shifting network of relationships, as long as you meet the precise and comprehensive set of metrics through which your performance is measured on a daily basis.

In the Green World, social responsibility is more than a buzzword. It is the ticket for doing business. Social media has created radical transparency in global companies, which societal pressures have pushed to become models of environmentally and socially sound practices. CEOs looking to drive "good growth" have spotlighted the HR function, since boosting employee morale and providing a work-life balance are considered top priorities throughout the business world. Your organization has steadily moved toward a flat, fluid structure where you are given more freedom to design your own role and goals to fit your lifestyle and personal passions. This raises a key challenge: in an organizational culture tailored to the needs of individual employees, how do you keep everyone on the same page? You find yourself needing to spend more and more time aligning around collective goals with your teammates and keeping in touch when everyone is able to make their own schedule.

In the Orange World, Silicon Valley–style entrepreneurialism is the rule rather than the exception. The concept of the full-time job is *so* last century. Networking technologies have made large, permanent organizational structures largely obsolete. Instead, highly specialized independent contractors or small companies come together to collaborate on a project-by-project basis. You might be building a website for one business in the morning and designing logos for another one in the afternoon. While you enjoy the freedom of working when and where you want to, you cringe at the need to gear up every time a new project starts. You have to form a new team with other contractors and entrepreneurs, some of whom you have never worked with before, and build rapport quickly so that you can deliver a product on time and on target. You rarely miss the old multinational you used to work for, but you do notice that you spend a lot more time on managing group dynamics than you ever did as a cubicle rat.

Which world do you think you will live in? Notice that in each case, technological and cultural changes will push you to focus more time and energy on managing team relationships. Whatever the world looks like in 2022, collaboration skills will be at a premium. Formal authority will be even less useful in motivating others. You will be even less able to rely on a unified company culture to keep everyone on the same page. Shifting work arrangements and networks will make it harder for you to fall back on long-term relationships with colleagues to get work done. In any scenario, then, it will take more effort to make shared commitments and stick to them. Good teamwork will be more relevant than ever as saying-doing gaps grow between co-workers and partners who move quickly from one project to the next.

So, how did you answer the question: Will your world be Blue, Green, or Orange? As far as collaboration goes, your answer leads to the same conclusion. You will have to spend *more* time on teamwork.

Teamwork Trends

Think further about these possibilities, and you might begin to see that the future is even more complex than you first imagined. Major sociocultural and technological trends will likely cause four significant changes in the way you collaborate with your teammates.

Flatter Teams

"Wait, what's a circle again?"

The last time you asked that question was in preschool. But then again, nothing about this group would surprise you right now. As you look around the meeting table, you are having trouble identifying a true team leader, because there is no leader. There is only a facilitator, who explains: "It's what we call teams now. This is the product development circle, remember? So, should we get started talking about our tensions? I have another tactical meeting with the sales circle to get to soon."

The person to your left pipes up: "I'm processing a tension about the new launch date. It's coming up, and I need more support on working out some of the bugs to hit our deadline." After the group helps your colleague identify a "lead link" in the research circle who could help her get debugging support, the next person raises his hand. "I have a tension about the kitchen. Nobody takes time to clean up after themselves and I've done the dishes for the past three days straight."

Circles? Tensions? Lead Links? If you are having trouble keeping up with the jargon, you can appreciate what the employees at companies like Zappos and Medium experienced when they first implemented the new collaborative process called Holacracy.[3] Created by programmer Brian Robertson, the system does away with management hierarchies in favor of flat, interconnected teams that assign roles and solve problems on the fly, through regular meetings. Productivity guru David Allen likes its relentless focus on adaptation and rapid decision making. Another appealing aspect: no middle management bottlenecks.

Holacracy is an extreme example of a shift in work relationships away from hierarchy and toward decentralized decision making. More and more businesses are gradually moving in this direction, spurred by a growing body of research and real world case studies demonstrating that empowering employees with more autonomy makes them more motivated and fosters a diversity of perspectives that often leads to better decisions. In Chapter 1, we introduced you to W.L. Gore and Associates, which was an early adopter of the "lattice" organizational structure, where small, interconnected teams of associates replace vertical chains of command. Having employees follow the guidance of mentor-like leaders rather than being supervised by managers has landed Gore on *Fortune* magazine's "100 Best Companies to Work For" list for the past three decades.

Teamwork Trends

Flatter

Rigid hierarchies and verticals are giving way to flat teams in organizations as diverse as Zappos, Gore, and Basecamp. You will likely have to work harder to manage horizontally as formal authority carries less clout.

Looser

The rise of the sharing economy, outsourcing, and freelancing mean that more of us will be attached to multiple teams across organizational boundaries. You will have to find ways to keep these groups on track with their goals and shared norms, even as individual members come and go.

Wider

Technology affords us new flexibility to connect with colleagues internationally. Your permanent team might be in an office across the country, but they are also a Skype call or chat message away. The challenges of communicating effectively with a virtual team could become your everyday reality.

Faster

More businesses are finding value in the Hollywood model of work, where loose networks of specialists come together rapidly to perform short-term projects and disband just as quickly, only to be reassembled on the next project. You will have to get better at building a team quickly and repeatedly.

At IDEO, employees are "invited" to attend meetings.[4] When they do, they expect the best idea in the room will win whether it comes from a new designer, or the CEO. Vice president Tom Kelley believes that this democratic atmosphere and the lack of a strict management structure are crucial to spurring the creativity his teams need to keep their innovation edge: "Innovation requires that we draw upon every single person in our organization for ideas. However, if there's a strict hierarchical system, people would have a hard time expressing their opinions since employees tend to want to please their superiors. It's important to flatten the organization and build a culture where everyone's idea is respected and where mistakes are allowed to happen."

Never one to shy away from walking the walk, Kelley has been mentored by employees 15 years his junior so he can get a different generational perspective on his work.

At the productivity software company Basecamp,[5] a rotating management system means each person will have to step into a leadership role at some point. This keeps team rapport high as it eliminates the management-labor tensions that create barriers to collaboration in many businesses.

Despite the benefits of the trend toward flatter teams, it also raises a host of new challenges. For example, Basecamp co-founder Jason Fried had to take an unusual step for his company when an employee complained about wanting new managerial responsibilities: he let her go—and this in spite of her being a top performer. She needed vertical mobility that the company could not provide. Misalignments around developmental goals such as this one are a key issue raised by flattened structures.

At Zappos, many employees value the high level of input they have under Holacracy. Under this system, even a shuttle bus driver was able to make it company policy to keep trash out of the vehicle. On the other hand, employees find that they spend more time and energy figuring out roles that can shift frequently as tasks are reallocated on the fly. At Gore, the model of having informal guides instead of managers means policy enforcement can be tough, since employees need to be self-motivated to adhere to company norms.

In sum, the trend toward more autonomy in teams has the potential to unlock vast reservoirs of employee energy and creativity, but it also creates a freewheeling environment in which it can be tougher to have a structured discussion about team commitments.

Looser Structure

It feels like a large-scale version of the garage where Jobs and Wozniak launched Apple. But actually, it is a co-working office. Mike looks out the windows of his conference room at the other independent designers and consultants whose workspaces are connected like pieces of a jigsaw puzzle. Professionals are chatting on iPhones with clients in all corners of the world, their conversations blending with the sounds of indie rock streaming over the wireless speakers hanging over his head.

Mike turns back to his colleague, a marketing specialist, who is soliciting ideas on a new company name from three entrepreneurs involved in a rebranding process. The specialist is wearing a faded black t-shirt and tan chinos, mirroring the laid-back fashion sense of his clients. After Mike wraps up this meeting, he will don a button-down shirt and a blazer for a presentation downtown at a corporate office. He will make sure to get there a little early to touch base with the representatives of the marketing firm that contracted with him to design logos for their client.

Like the other independent professionals with whom he shares a co-working space, Mike values the independence of being a freelancer. But he sometimes feels far from free, because he spends so much of his time managing relationships with the different partners and companies in his network.

Mike represents a significant trend: the rise of contingent labor. By 2020, freelancers and temps are expected to make up 20 percent of the workforce,[6] up from about 15 percent today. While temp agencies have provided staffing solutions since their rise in the 1950s, companies like Taskrabbit are reducing the role of the middleman and connecting companies directly with freelancers. These modern-day temps run errands and perform quick services, but a growing number of businesses like MBA and Company are offering high-level consulting talent to staff entire strategy and operations projects.

This trend has been driven in part by a weaker economy in which employers are more able to maintain flexible workforces to raise efficiency and keep overhead low. But workers are also driving the trend: millennials tend to value the independence and flexibility of freelancing. Ironically, as workers become more independent, social networks become denser and teams become more ubiquitous.

Wider Connections

Your alarm rings at 2:45 A.M. You shake yourself awake and shuffle down the hall to your home office. Luckily, since the call with your Shanghai colleagues is audio only, you can wait to get dressed. The rest of your day's schedule will be spent on calls and videoconferences with other partners and clients in San Francisco, Chicago, New York, and Atlanta. Your work has become unmoored from geography. You can do your work anywhere, and travel whenever a face-to-face meeting or facilitation is really necessary.

In this globalized, highly connected world, as many as 50 million Americans—40 percent of the workforce—work from home at least part of the time.[7] Approximately 48 percent of all managers spend half of their week working remotely (from home or on the road). Since co-location is rarely required to get work done, it makes sense not to commute daily to a building filled with offices and cubicles where everyone communicates through email and phone anyway. Proponents of telecommuting tout the cost savings to companies that do not need large office spaces to support their workforce.

But robust telecommuting arrangements have a dark side, too. Always open on your desktop are two windows: your email that you are constantly refreshing, and your company's chat application. Since you work mostly from home and on the road, you feel a need to be always available and visible to the rest of your team members.

Another drawback is the pressure to put in "virtual face time." A study conducted by Boston University professor Erin Reid[8] revealed a major division among the staff at a global consulting firm. Some were clearly seen as being less committed and lower achievers whereas others were viewed as star performers. The difference? Consultants in the first group had formally requested flexible schedules to take care of their families and handle other affairs at home. The "star performers" asked for no time off, but they actually worked fewer hours—50 or 60 rather than the standard 80. They just found ways to make it seem like they were always working. For example, they would strategically send an email or two at odd hours. Those who were known to be working from home were only *perceived* to be less productive than their colleagues who never bothered to tell anyone about the arrangement.

Other studies reveal that those who work remotely are often even more productive than their office-bound counterparts.[9] Research conducted by the Chinese travel website Ctrip showed that employees working from home made 13.5 percent more calls—almost a whole extra workday's worth of productivity per week.

As wide teams become the norm, you will need to learn how to contend with a few distinctive challenges: the challenge of working and being "virtually visible" at all hours; the challenge of conveying the impression when you work remotely that you are busy and productive, even though you are actually *more* busy and productive than your co-workers in the office; and, of course, the challenge of teaming with geographically dispersed co-workers who are on multiple teams in multiple time zones.

Faster Work

"Anything—a misremembered line, an extra step taken,[10] a camera operator stumbling on a stair or veering off course or out of focus—could blow a take, rendering the first several minutes unusable even if they had been perfect. You had to be word-perfect, you had to be on script, and you literally had to count your paces down to the number of steps you needed to take before turning a corner."

So Michael Keaton described the incredibly stressful experience of making *Birdman*. It was filmed to look like one long, continuous shot. Actors did 10- to 12-minute takes that had to flow perfectly to be usable. Under Alejandro González Iñárritu's direction, a team of actors and craftsmen came together to shoot this award-winning film (four Academy Awards, including best picture in 2015) in fewer than 30 days.

This is the so-called Hollywood model of working. Get used to it. Here is what you can expect: an opportunity is identified and a team is assembled that works together only as long as it takes to finish a project. You might collaborate with some people on multiple assignments, but on each one you have to re-form a team only to dissolve it again a few weeks later.

In more and more businesses, the Hollywood model is applied to fixed-term projects that are large and complex, requiring a number of differentiated, complementary skill sets. The last hundred years or so of enterprise have been based on the manufacturing model. But no longer. "More of us will see our working lives structured around short-term,[11] project-based teams, rather than long-term, open-ended jobs," NPR's Adam Davidson predicts.

As work becomes faster, Hollywood style, your ability to be a flexible, committed, high-performing teammate will determine whether you work at all.

Your Toolbox for the Hyper-Collaborative World

Now you have seen the future of teamwork: flatter, looser, wider, faster. Are you prepared? Not to worry. We know you are prepared, because you know how to apply the 3x3 Framework (Figure C.1).

A quick review shows that the 3x3 Framework will help you:

Figure C.1

Establish Commitments   Every team—now and in the future—needs to make commitments in the form of goals, roles, and norms. Team members will need to be honest with themselves and each other about their abilities and their competing commitments. One of your team's greatest assets will be a high-performing culture, which promotes the adaptability and flexibility needed in the hyper-collaborative physical and virtual worlds.

Check Alignment   Teams have always drifted from their initial commitments. The pushes and pulls that cause drift will only continue to multiply as work becomes flatter, looser, wider, and faster. Fortunately, teammates will help get projects back on course when they have been properly prepared to identify and address misalignments.

Close the Saying-Doing Gap   Successful teams are disciplined about developing habits that support their commitments. In the early twentieth century, William James said that habits are the great flywheel of society. That same flywheel will continue powering the age of digital communication, wide teams, and project-based work.

Passion and Performance through Process

But wait—you are already living in the hypercollaborative world. As William Gibson, the cyperpunk novelist, once said,[12] "The future is already here. It's just not evenly distributed yet."

Entire organizations are structured like a high-performing team that works flatter, looser, wider, and faster. Just consider Salesforce.com. Starting with a customer resource management (CRM) product that was launched in 1999, Salesforce.com has grown to become one of the most highly valued cloud computing companies in the world. Somehow, as this company grew from a startup to an organization of 10,000 employees and a market capitalization of over $50 billion, it has been able to maintain a strong culture of innovation. Under the leadership of founder Mark Benioff, it has avoided the usual pitfalls of startup success: a ballooning bureaucracy, limited flexibility, and flagging passion.

Salesforce.com has retained its startup energy by adopting the SCRUM technique of teaming. SCRUM was originally developed in the 1980s by game developers, Hirotaka Takeuchi and Ikujiro Nonaka, to increase speed and agility on product development teams. It values innovation and shared responsibility among all members of a cross-functional team. Management gurus Ken Schwaber and Jeff Sutherland[13] adapted the idea to general business practices, and it has steadily gained popularity in many organizations. To truly and successfully implement SCRUM requires a mindset in which managers are enablers rather than enforcers. Workers also have to see themselves differently: self-organizing and accountable rather than simply following the lead of their bosses.

An over-the-top commitment to clear structure supports flexibility. Benioff's V2MOM system[14] (vision, values, methods, obstacles, and measures) maps out every product and to-do in the company, from large product launches to the weekly office grocery list. Employees have personal to-do lists that they use to track their progress quarterly. For projects that are high-priority, an internal CEO is assigned, and given as many resources as necessary. This system exemplifies the 3x3 principles: it clearly lays out commitments, creates a process for check-ins, and helps to minimize the saying-doing gap. Even further, it helps ignites passion among workers.

At an annual internal job fair, employees are encouraged to shop around for opportunities. No one should feel "stuck," or locked in to just one job. "Any job you do long enough, it starts to get a bit boring, and I was told to explore," said Leyla Seka, a manager of Salesforce's App Exchange.[15] Retaining workers who are excited and passionate has helped to supercharge the company. As of 2015, Salesforce.com had won *Forbes'* Most Innovative Company Award three years running. Other achievements: some of the highest customer satisfaction ratings in the industry and a sector-leading stock price.

Benioff has already ushered his Salesforce.com teams into the hyper-collaborative world. With the tools in this book, you can bring your team there, too.

So What About You?

Let's end by imagining how you might take a small step toward putting the 3x3 Framework into action. And since the process is iterative—not a linear, one-time event—let's loop back to where we started at the beginning of this book ...

... With the sweat still dripping down your face. Your hands are cramping from pulling on the rope with all your might. You look up and the boulder attached to the rope is still there, still stubbornly in place. Your fellow team members begin piling on to join you. After all, as soon as you haul the rock 30 feet, you all get to leave the company retreat and head to a celebratory team dinner.

Only this time you stop everyone from blindly grabbing the rope and yanking. Perplexed, your teammates gather around as you ask what the team's goal should be. "Obviously to get the rock across the finish line," someone offers. But you keep pressing. When you start asking about the roles and norms that will best achieve that goal, you see ah-ha looks appearing.

Rather than having everyone pull at random, you decide to yank the rope in unison. You put the strongest team members closest to the rock and assign the most outgoing team member to be the motivator, going up and down the line making sure everyone is engaged.

Energized, the team begins pulling. But after a few seconds, the motivator realizes that the rock could be moving faster. He suggests corrections to the team's pulling technique that create better leverage. After the team makes the change, the rock begins moving quickly and steadily forward. Once it crosses the mark, everyone cheers, having conquered the social loafing barrier that had been plaguing the team.

"Maybe teams can work after all," you say to yourself as you wipe the sweat off your brow. You join the others as they walk off the field and head to dinner. It feels good to know that you are finally, fully a ... *committed team*.

ACKNOWLEDGMENTS

This book was a team effort. We are indebted to numerous contributors, supporters, and advocates who made it possible.

The insights that drove this book were co-created with our contributing authors: Joanne, Vishal, Amy, Lauren, Michael, Annette, and Renee, all of whom have been part of our own team at Wharton Executive Education from the beginning. The 3×3 framework is a product of our collective thinking and practice. We engaged in countless discussions, debates, and jam sessions around Mario's kitchen table. Our team was truly committed.

Our partner Joe Perfetti played an essential role. He always gave us the time we needed to write, even under the pressure of demanding schedules. He also provided invaluable opportunities to reality-test our thinking at every stage.

We are grateful to Pete Fader and Dave Heckman at Wharton for supporting our HPT process right from the get-go.

Our editor, Richard Narramore, provided timely feedback that pushed our writing toward even greater clarity at crucial junctures.

Our research assistant Aaisha Gulani mined the library for teamwork stories that helped bring our insights to life.

Last, but certainly not least, we thank our families.

Mario's home team—Robin, Miles, Ella, and Bix—provided unwavering support throughout the writing process. With exquisite grace, they listened, questioned, and nudged. Mario owes his family an enormous debt of gratitude.

Derek's wife, Carrie, patiently gave him space for Sunday morning drafting sessions while prodding him to take much-needed dinner breaks on Philadelphia's 13th Street corridor. His parents, Christine and Emily, provided plenty of encouragement and advice in weekend calls from Portland, Oregon.

Madeline's family—Mom, Dad, Corinne, and Barbara—though dispersed across the globe, never failed to pick up the phone when she needed to vent, brainstorm, and celebrate milestones. Her other circle of loved ones—Chris, Lulu, Mariam, and Juls—made sure to push back when needed and never allowed her to take herself too seriously. For that, she is eternally grateful.

NOTES

Introduction

1. The original research publicizing the concept of social loafing is M. Ringelmann (1913), "Recherches sur les moteurs animés: Travail de l'homme" [Research on animate sources of power: The work of man], *Annales de l'Institut National Agronomique*, 2nd series, vol. 12, 1–40. Available online (in French) at http://gallica.bnf.fr/ark:/12148/bpt6k54409695.image.f14 .langEN.

2. The graduation speech delivered by David Foster Wallace to the 2005 graduating class of Kenyon College is available at http://bulletin.kenyon.edu/x4276 .html.

3. For more details on this study and a comprehensive look at the question of how effective we are in reading the minds of others, see Nicholas Epley, *Mindwise: Why We Misunderstand What Others Think, Believe, Feel, and Want* (New York: Vintage Books, 2014).

4. From Clifford Geertz, "The Impact of the Concept of Culture on the Concept of Man," Chapter 2 in *The Interpretation of Cultures: Selected Essays* (New York: Basic Books, 1973), 9.

5. For a comprehensive overview of Hackman's writing on working in teams and group dynamics, see J. Richard Hackman, *Leading Teams: Setting the Stage for Great Performances* (Boston: Harvard Business School Publishing, 2002). Our HPT observer team relied heavily on Hackman's research in developing our own framework of evaluation for Wharton EDP.

6. James Detert and Amy C. Edmondson, "Why Employees Are Afraid to Speak," *Harvard Business Review*, 85, no. 5 (2007): 23–25. https://hbr.org/ 2007/05/why-employees-are-afraid-to-speak.

Chapter 1

1. Our description of Alan Turing and the Hut 8 team is drawn from two works: Andrew Hodges and Douglas Hofstadter, *Alan Turing: The Enigma: The Book That Inspired the Film* The Imitation Game (Princeton, NJ: Princeton University Press, 2014); and Nigel Farndale, "The Imitation Game: Who Were the Real Bletchley Park Codebreakers?" *The Telegraph,* November 14, 2014, www.telegraph.co.uk/culture/film/film-news/11229240/The-Imitation-Game-who-were-the-real-Bletchley-Park-codebreakers.html.

2. For more details on the movie, see IMDb's write-up at: www.imdb.com/title/tt2084970/.

3. See Leigh Thompson, *Creative Conspiracy: The New Rules of Breakthrough Collaboration* (Boston: Harvard Business Review Press, 2013).

4. See Morten Hansen, *Collaboration: How Leaders Avoid the Traps, Build Common Ground, and Reap Big Results* (Boston: Harvard Business Review Press, 2009).

5. See Clifford Geertz, *The Interpretation of Cultures; Selected Essays* (New York: Basic Books, 1973).

6. Heidi Halvorson writes about personal goal-setting—and how it is a defining habit of successful people—in *Nine Things Successful People Do Differently* (Boston: Harvard Business Review Press, 2011), and if/then thinking in team settings in "Get Your Team to Do What It Says It's Going to Do," *Harvard Business Review*, May 2014, available online at https://hbr.org/2014/05/get-your-team-to-do-what-it-says-its-going-to-do.

7. See David Allen, *Getting Things Done: The Art of Stress-Free Productivity*, reprint edition (New York: Penguin Group, 2002).

8. See Chapter 2: "A Real Team" in Hackman's book, *Leading Teams,* for a full discussion of co-acting groups versus real teams.

9. Amy Wrzesniewski and Jane E. Dutton, "Crafting a Job: Revisioning Employees as Active Crafters of Their Work," *Academy of Management Review* 26, no. 2 (2001), 179–201. http://doi.org/10.5465/AMR.2001.4378011.

10. See Tim Kastelle, "Hierarchy Is Overrated," *Harvard Business Review,* November 20, 2013, https://hbr.org/2013/11/hierarchy-is-overrated/.

11. See Andy Boynton and Bill Fischer, *Virtuoso Teams: Lessons from Teams that Changed Their Worlds* (Harlow, UK; New York: Financial Times–Prentice Hall, 2005).

12. See Joshua Wolf Shenk, "The Power of Two," *The Atlantic*, July/August 2014. Available online at www.theatlantic.com/features/archive/2014/06/the-power-of-two/372289/.

13. See Jonah Weiner, "Paul McCartney Can't Slow Down," *Rolling Stone*, October 23, 2013, http://www.rollingstone.com/music/news/paul-mccartney-cant-slow-down-inside-rolling-stones-new-cover-story-20131023.

14. See G. Richard Shell and Mario Moussa, *The Art of Woo: Using Strategic Persuasion to Sell Your Ideas*, reprint edition (New York: Penguin Group, 2008).

15. See Cass R. Sunstein and Reid Hastie, "Making Dumb Groups Smarter," *Harvard Business Review* 92, no. 12 (2014): 90–98.

16. We draw from Diana Peterson's interview with Glen Mazzara for this story: http://hollywoodwritersoffice.blogspot.com/2009/07/interview-hawthorne-executive-producer.html.

17. See Sheryl Sandberg and Adam Grant, "Sheryl Sandberg and Adam Grant on Why Women Stay Quiet at Work," *New York Times,* January 12, 2015, www.nytimes.com/2015/01/11/opinion/sunday/speaking-while-female.html

Chapter 2

1. See Diane Coutu, "A Reading List for Bill Gates—and You: A Conversation with Literary Critic Harold Bloom," *Harvard Business Review,* May 2001.

2. Rappaport's research on the Maring tribe of Papua, New Guinea, originally published in 1984, was released as a second edition in 2000. Harold A. Rappaport, *Pigs for the Ancestors: Ritual in the Ecology of a New Guinea People* (Long Grove, IL: Waveland Press, 2000).

3. See Kurt Eichenwald, "Microsoft's Lost Decade," *Vanity Fair,* August 2012, www.vanityfair.com/news/business/2012/08/microsoft-lost-mojo-steve-ballmer.

4. See Clifford Geertz, *The Interpretation of Cultures: Selected Essays* (New York: Basic Books, 1973).

5. See Jennifer Reingold, Marty Jones, and Susan Kramer, "How to Fail in Business While Really, Really Trying," *Fortune,* March 20, 2014, http://fortune.com/2014/03/20/how-to-fail-in-business-while-really-really-trying/.

6. Cultural psychologist Thomas Talhelm is credited for leading the study on what is known as "the rice theory;" the idea that communities growing rice,

especially those of the East, tend to foster cultures that are more cooperative and interconnected. To read more about his research findings, see Thomas Talhelm et al., "Large-Scale Psychological Differences within China Explained by Rice versus Wheat Agriculture," *Science* 344, no. 6184 (2014): 603–604. www.sciencemag.org/content/344/6184/603.

7. See Elizabeth K. Briody et al., *Transforming Culture: Creating and Sustaining a Better Manufacturing Organization* (New York: Palgrave Macmillan, 2010).

8. The details of this tragic incident were drawn from extensive reporting in: Phil LeBeau and Jeff Pohlman, "The Corporate Culture: Behind the Scenes at General Motors," CNBC, aired/published May 16, 2014, www.cnbc.com/id/101673363; Max Nisen, "The Culture That Made the Whole of GM Miss One Engineer's Fatal Mistake," *Quartz,* June 6, 2014, http://qz.com/217705/the-culture-that-made-the-whole-of-gm-miss-one-engineers-fatal-mistake/; Barry Meier and Hilary Stout, "Victims of G.M. Deadly Defect Fall Through Legal Cracks," *New York Times,* December 29, 2014, www.nytimes.com/2014/12/30/business/victims-of-gm-deadly-defect-fall-through-legal-cracks.html.

9. See Max H. Bazerman and Ann E. Tenbrunsel, "Ethical Breakdowns," *Harvard Business Review* 89, no. 4 (April 2011): 58–65, https://hbr.org/2011/04/ethical-breakdowns.

10. Again, see Bazerman and Tenbrunsel's "Ethical Breakdowns."

11. See Upton Sinclair, *I, Candidate for Governor: And How I Got Licked* (Oakland: University of California Press, 1935 (1994)).

12. See Emre Soyer and Robin M. Hogarth, "Fooled by Experience," *Harvard Business Review* 93, no. 5 (2015): 72–77, https://hbr.org/2015/05/fooled-by-experience.

13. See Jon Krakauer, *Into Thin Air: A Personal Account of the Mt. Everest Disaster*, (Princeton, NJ: Anchor, 1999).

14. This concept of psychological safety comes from Amy C. Edmondson, *Teaming: How Organizations Learn, Innovate, and Compete in the Knowledge Economy* (San Francisco: Jossey-Bass, 2012).

15. See Anita Woolley, Thomas W. Malone, and Christopher F. Chabris, "Why Some Teams Are Smarter Than Others," *New York Times,* January 16, 2015, www.nytimes.com/2015/01/18/opinion/sunday/why-some-teams-are-smarter-than-others.html.

16. See Howard S. Becker, *Outsiders: Studies in the Sociology of Deviance* (New York: The Free Press, 1963).

17. See Robert Hogan and Robert B. Kaiser, "What We Know about Leadership," *Review of General Psychology* 9, no. 2 (2005): 169–180.

18. See George Kohlrieser, Susan Goldsworthy, and Duncan Coombe, *Care to Dare: Unleashing Astonishing Potential through Secure Base Leadership* (San Francisco: Jossey-Bass, 2012).

19. Christopher J. Roussin, "Increasing Trust, Psychological Safety, and Team Performance through Dyadic Leadership Discovery," *Small Group Research* 39, no. 2 (2008): 224–248, http://doi.org/10.1177/1046496408315988.

20. For a comprehensive explanation of Shell's bargaining styles, we recommend his book G. Richard Shell, *Bargaining for Advantage: Negotiation Strategies for Reasonable People* (New York: Penguin Books, 2000).

Chapter 3

1. See Charles Duhigg, *The Power of Habit: Why We Do What We Do in Life and Business* (New York: Random House, 2014).

2. See Mica Pollock, "From Shallow to Deep: Toward a Thorough Cultural Analysis of School Achievement Patterns," *Anthropology & Education Quarterly* 39, no. 4 (2008): 369–380.

3. The full speech can be read or listened to at: www.jfklibrary.org/Research/Research-Aids/JFK-Speeches/United-States-Congress-Special-Message_19610525.aspx.

4. See Walter A. McDougall, *The Heavens and the Earth: A Political History of the Space Age* (Baltimore: Johns Hopkins University Press, 1985).

5. See Brian Mockenhaupt, "Fire on the Mountain," *The Atlantic,* June 2014, www.theatlantic.com/features/archive/2014/05/fire-on-the-mountain/361613/.

6. See Free Vogelstein, *Dogfight: How Apple and Google Went to War and Started a Revolution* (New York: Sarah Crichton Books, 2013).

7. Roger M. Schwarz, *The Skilled Facilitator: A Comprehensive Resource for Consultants, Facilitators, Managers, Trainers, and Coaches*, 2nd ed. (San Francisco: Jossey-Bass, 2002).

8. Susan Cain, *Quiet: The Power of Introverts in a World That Can't Stop Talking* (New York: Broadway Books, 2013).

9. Amy C. Edmondson, "Managing the Risk of Learning: Psychological Safety in Work Teams," *International Handbook of Organizational Teamwork and*

Cooperative Working, April 16, 2008, http://onlinelibrary.wiley.com/doi/10
.1002/9780470696712.ch13/summary.

10. Gabriele Oettingen, professor of psychology at New York University, is
credited with introducing the concept of "mental contrasting." For more
information, visit www.psych.nyu.edu/oettingen/.

11. Covey covers the concept of "urgent" versus "important" in his best-selling
The 7 Habits of Highly Effective People: Powerful Lessons of Personal Change
(New York: Simon & Schuster, 1989). Specifically, he covers these concepts in
"Habit 3: Put First Things First."

12. See page 139 of Steve Martin, *Born Standing Up: A Comic's Life* (New York:
Scribner, 2007).

13. See page 6 of Mark McClusky, *Faster, Higher, Stronger: How Sports Science Is
Creating a New Generation of Superathletes—and What We Can Learn from
Them* (New York: Hudson Street Press, 2014).

14. Goldsmith elaborates on the concept of "feedforward" at his website: www
.marshallgoldsmithlibrary.com/cim/articles_display.php?aid=110.

15. See Richard H. Thaler and Cass R. Sunstein, *Nudge: Improving Decisions About
Health, Wealth, and Happiness* (New York: Penguin Group, 2008).

16. Atul Gawande, *The Checklist Manifesto: How to Get Things Right* (New York:
Metropolitan Books, 2009).

17. Erez Yoeli, Syon Bhanot, Gordon Kraft-Todd, and David Rand, "How to Get
People to Pitch In," *New York Times,* May 15, 2015, www.nytimes.com/2015/
05/17/opinion/sunday/how-to-get-people-to-pitch-in.html.

18. "Productive paranoia" is discussed in Collins's book *Great by Choice: Uncertainty, Chaos, and Luck—Why Some Thrive Despite Them All,* authored with
Morten T. Hansen (New York: HarperCollins, 2011).

19. Bandura's ideas are discussed by Heidi Grant Halvorson in "Being an Optimist
without Being a Fool," *Harvard Business Review,* May 2, 2011, https://hbr.org/
2011/05/be-an-optimist-without-being-a/.

20. See page 22 of Caroline L. Arnold, *Small Move, Big Change: Using Microresolutions to Transform Your Life Permanently* (New York: Penguin Group, 2014).

21. Eric Ries, *The Lean Startup: How Today's Entrepreneurs Use Continuous
Innovation to Create Radically Successful Businesses* (New York: Crown Business,
2011).

22. James, described as the father of American psychology, defined "habit" in *The
Principles of Psychology,* published in 1890. The full quote is: "Habit is thus the

enormous flywheel of society, its most precious conservative agent. It alone is what keeps us all within the bounds of ordinance, and saves the children of fortune from the envious uprisings of the poor."

23. The quote is from Will Durant, "Chapter II: Aristotle and Greek Science; part VII: Ethics and the Nature of Happiness," in *The Story of Philosophy: The Lives and Opinions of the World's Greatest Philosophers* (New York: Simon & Schuster, 1926), 76.

Chapter 4

1. General Stanley McChrystal, Tantum Collins, David Silverman, and Chris Fussell, *Team of Teams: New Rules of Engagement for a Complex World* (New York: Portfolio, 2015).

2. Again, see McChrystal's account in *Team of Teams*.

3. Michael Lee, "Andre Iguodala, David Lee Took Back Seat So Warriors Could Flourish," *The Washington Post*, March 3, 2015, www.washingtonpost.com/ news/sports/wp/2015/03/03/andre-iguodala-david-lee-took-back-seat-so- warriors-could-flourish/.

4. For this story we draw from an oral history of the 2004 "Dream Team," as reported by Nate Penn, "Dunk'd," *GQ*, July 27, 2012, www.gq.com/story/ 2004-olympic-basketball-dream-team.

5. Natalia M. Lorinkova, Matthew J. Pearsall, and Henry P. Sims Jr., "Examining the Differential Longitudinal Performance of Directive versus Empowering Leadership in Teams," *Academy of Management Journal* 56, no. 2 (2013): 573–596, http://doi.org/10.5465/amj.2011.0132.

6. Lim is interviewed for the Corner Office feature of the *New York Times* by Sonia Kolesnikov-Jessop, "Building Teams by Winning Hearts and Minds," *New York Times*, June 7, 2015, www.nytimes.com/2015/06/08/business/ international/building-teams-by-winning-hearts-and-minds.html.

7. For more on the bean grinding initiative, see Julie Jargon, "At Starbucks, It's Back to the Grind," *Wall Street Journal*, June 17, 2009, www.wsj.com/articles/ SB124517480498919731; and Bruce Horovitz, "Starbucks Going Back to Grinding Beans," *USA Today*, March 19, 2008, http://usatoday30.usatoday .com/money/industries/food/2008-03-18-starbucks-changes_N.htm.

8. For a more in-depth understanding of VUCA, read "What VUCA Really Means for You," by Nathan Bennett and G. James Lemoine, *Harvard Business*

Review, January–February 2014: https://hbr.org/2014/01/what-vuca-really-means-for-you.

9. For details on his role in founding Team 6, see his book, *Rogue Warrior* (Delran, NJ: Simon & Schuster, 2009).

10. Mark Mazzetti, Nicholas Kulish, Christoper Drew, Serge F. Kovaleski, Sean D. Naylor, and John Ismay, "SEAL Team 6: A Secret History of Quiet Killings and Blurred Lines," *New York Times,* June 6, 2015, www.nytimes.com/2015/06/07/world/asia/the-secret-history-of-seal-team-6.html.

11. Details on the Drexler story were drawn from Steven Davidoff Solomon, "J. Crew Struggles With Its 'Great Man' Dilemma," *New York Times,* June 10, 2015, www.nytimes.com/2015/06/11/business/dealbook/j-crew-struggles-with-its-great-man-dilemma.html; Leslie Kaufman, "Gap's Chief Executive Unexpectedly Calls It Quits," *New York Times*, May 22, 2002, www.nytimes.com/2002/05/22/business/gap-s-chief-executive-unexpectedly-calls-it-quits.html; and Meryl Gordon, "Mickey Drexler's Redemption," *New York* magazine, November 22, 2004, http://nymag.com/nymetro/news/bizfinance/biz/features/10489/index3.html

12. Anita Woolley, Thomas W. Malone, and Christopher F. Chabris, "Why Some Teams Are Smarter Than Others," *New York Times,* January 16, 2015, www.nytimes.com/2015/01/18/opinion/sunday/why-some-teams-are-smarter-than-others.html.

Chapter 5

1. See Vijay Govindarajan and Anil K. Gupta, "Building an Effective Global Business Team," *MIT Sloan Management Review,* July 15, 2001, http://sloanreview.mit.edu/article/building-an-effective-global-business-team/.

2. This study is cited in the article "Getting Virtual Teams Right," written by Keith Ferrazzi for the December 2014 issue of the *Harvard Business Review*, https://hbr.org/2014/12/getting-virtual-teams-right.

3. The full article published by *Forbes,* June 29, 2011, www.forbes.com/sites/ccl/2011/06/29/flexibility-can-boost-employee-productivity/.

4. This study was published by the Center for Work and Family, which is part of Boston College. The full report can be downloaded at https://www.bc.edu/content/dam/files/centers/cwf/research/publications/pdf/BCCWF_Flex_Impact_Final_Report.pdf.

5. For more details on the differences between cognitive and affective trust, see Sean Graber's full *Harvard Business Review* article, published March 20, 2015, https://hbr.org/2015/03/why-remote-work-thrives-in-some-companies-and-fails-in-others.

6. You can view Coby's full speech online at http://devslovebacon.com/conferences/bacon-2014/talks/remote-by-default-how-github-makes-working-remotely-not-suck.

7. Again, Sean Graber's *Harvard Business Review* article, cited in note 6, is the source for this story.

8. Marcel Mauss, *The Gift: Forms and Functions of Exchange in Archaic Societies* (London: Routledge, 1990, 1922).

9. See Adam M. Grant, *Give and Take: Why Helping Others Drives Our Success* (New York: Penguin Books, 2013).

10. Again, Cody's speech at the BACON conference was the source for this quote (note 6).

11. Jacquelyn Smith wrote about this study for *Forbes* magazine, "How Millennials Work Differently from Everyone Else," published September 13, 2012, www.forbes.com/sites/jacquelynsmith/2012/09/13/how-millennials-work-differently-from-everyone-else/.

12. See Farhad Manjoo, "Slack, the Office Messaging App that May Finally Sink Email," *New York Times,* March 11, 2015, www.nytimes.com/2015/03/12/technology/slack-the-office-messaging-app-that-may-finally-sink-email.html

13. The *New York Times* article by Farhad Manjoo cited earlier (Note 12) is the source for this quote.

14. You can view the full *Key and Peele* skit on Comedy Central's website: www.cc.com/video-clips/1nwt2i/key-and-peele-text-message-confusion---uncensored.

15. The full story (audio and text) by Emma Bowman, aired May 4, 2015, is available on NPR's website: www.npr.org/sections/alltechconsidered/2015/05/04/404209790/as-emoji-spread-beyond-texts-many-remain-confounded-face-interrobang.

16. See Jason Fried and David Heinemeier Hansson, *Remote: Office Not Required* (New York: Crown Publishing Group, 2013).

17. The Yahoo! memo was published by *All Things Digital,* an online publication specializing in technology and startup company news and a member of the *Wall Street Journal*'s Digital Network. The Yahoo! memo is still posted at

http://allthingsd.com/20130222/physically-together-heres-the-internal-yahoo-no-work-from-home-memo-which-extends-beyond-remote-workers/.

Chapter 6

1. See Adam Lashinsky, "How Dollar Shave Club Got Started," *Fortune,* March 20, 2015, http://fortune.com/2015/03/10/dollar-shave-club-founding/.

2. See Biz Stone's own words ("Twitter's Co-founder on Creating Opportunities"), as published by *Harvard Business Review,* June 2015 : https://hbr.org/2015/06/twitters-cofounder-on-creating-opportunities.

3. See Julie Livingston, *Founders at Work: Stories of Startups' Early Days* (Berkeley, CA: Apress, 2009).

4. For more on the story of the founding of Excite, see Livingston's *Founders at Work,* cited earlier (note 3).

5. For more on Seligmann's research on resilience, see his article, "Building Resilience," April 2011, *Harvard Business Review*, https://hbr.org/2011/04/building-resilience.

6. See Adam Lashinsky, "Uber: An Oral History," *Fortune,* June 3, 2015, http://fortune.com/2015/06/03/uber-an-oral-history/.

7. See Tim Bradshaw, "Lunch with the FT: Brian Chesky," *Financial Times,* December 26, 2014, www.ft.com/intl/cms/s/0/fd685212-8768-11e4-bc7c-00144feabdc0.html.

8. Read more on Tim Brady's experience at Yahoo! in Livingston's *Founders at Work,* cited earlier (note 3).

9. The concept of the "yellow flag" is discussed in Jeremy Bloom's book, *Fueled by Failure: Using Detours and Defeats to Power Progress* (Irvine, CA: Entrepreneur Press, 2015).

10. For more on the founding of Pinterest, see Simon Baribeau's article, "The Pinterest Pivot," *Fast Company,* October 23, 2013, www.fastcompany.com/3001984/pinterest-pivot.

11. The story of the Kodak Gallery pivot is adapted from Eric Ries's book, *The Lean Startup: How Today's Entrepreneurs Use Continuous Innovation to Create Radically Successful Businesses* (New York: Crown Business, 2011).

Chapter 7

1. Judd Apatow, *Sick in the Head: Conversations about Life and Comedy* (New York: Random House, 2015).

2. Steve Johnson, *Where Good Ideas Come From*, (New York: Riverhead Books, 2011).

3. See the case study by Henry W. Chesbrough, Sohyeong Kim, and Alice Agogino, "Chez Panisse: Building an Open Innovation Ecosystem," *Harvard Business Review*, June 30, 2014, https://hbr.org/product/chez-panisse-building-an-open-innovation-ecosystem/an/B5806-PDF-ENG.

4. See Beth Kowitt, "How Ikea Took Over the World," *Fortune* 171, no. 4 (2015): 166–175.

5. R. E. Dugan and K. J. Gabriel, "'Special Forces' Innovation: How DARPA Attacks Problems," *Harvard Business Review* 91, no. 10 (2013): 74–84.

6. See Robert A. Guth, "In Secret Hideaway, Bill Gates Ponders Microsoft's Future," *Wall Street Journal—Eastern Edition* 245, no. 60 (March 28, 2005): A1–A13.

7. See Thomas McNamee, *Alice Waters and Chez Panisse*, (New York: Penguin Books, 2008).

8. Again, see "Special Forces," cited earlier (note 5).

9. See Julie Livingston, *Founders at Work: Stories of Startups' Early Days* (Berkeley, CA: Apress, 2009).

10. See Kowitt's *Fortune* article on IKEA, cited earlier (note 4).

11. See Bruce Nussbaum, *Creative Intelligence: Harnessing the Power to Create, Connect, and Inspire* (New York: HarperBusiness, 2013).

12. Christian Terwiesch and Karl Ulrich, *Innovation Tournaments: Creating and Selecting Exceptional Opportunities* (Boston: Harvard Business Review Press, 2009).

13. See the discussion in Drew Boyd and Jacob Goldenberg, *Inside the Box: A Proven System of Creativity for Breakthrough Results*, reprint edition (New York: Simon & Schuster, 2014).

14. You can view this Monty Python skit on YouTube at https://www.youtube.com/watch?v=ogPZ5CY9KoM.

15. George Plimpton, "John Gregory Dunne, the Art of Screenwriting No. 2," *Paris Review* 138 (Spring 1996), www.theparisreview.org/interviews/1430/the-art-of-screenwriting-no-2-john-gregory-dunne.

16. Jonah Weiner, "Comedy Central in the Post-TV Era," *New York Times,* June 18, 2015, www.nytimes.com/2015/06/21/magazine/comedy-central-in-the-post-tv-era.html.

17. Keith Richards and James Fox, *Life,* (New York: Back Bay Books, 2011).

18. Again, see Nussbaum's book, *Creative Intelligence,* cited earlier (note 11).

19. Matthew Dollinger, "Starbucks, 'The Third Place,' and Creating the Ultimate Customer Experience," *Fast Company,* June 11, 2008, www.fastcompany.com/887990/starbucks-third-place-and-creating-ultimate-customer-experience.

20. Steven Johnson, *Where Good Ideas Come From,* (New York: Riverhead Books, 2011).

21. Again, see Apatow's book, *Sick in the Head,* cited earlier (note 1).

22. Again, see Nussbaum's book, *Creative Intelligence,* cited earlier (note 11).

Chapter 8

1. Chase Morsey Jr., *The Man Who Saved the V-8: The Untold Stories of Some of the Most Important Product Decisions in the History of Ford Motor Company* (North Charleston, SC: CreateSpace Independent Publishing Platform, 2014).

2. Daniel Kahneman, *Thinking, Fast and Slow,* (New York: Farrar, Straus and Giroux, 2013).

3. Thomas Bonsall, *Disaster in Dearborn: The Story of the Edsel* (Redwood City, CA: Stanford University Press, 2002); and John Brooks, *Business Adventures: Twelve Classic Tales from the World of Wall Street* (New York: Open Road Integrated Media, 2014).

4. Karen A. Brown, Nancy Lea Hyer, and Richard Ettenson, "The Question Every Project Team Should Answer," *MIT Sloan Management Review,* September 11, 2013, http://sloanreview.mit.edu/article/the-question-every-project-team-should-answer/.

5. Anneloes M.L. Raes, Heike Bruch, and Simon B. De Jong, "How Top Management Team Behavioural Integration Can Impact Employee Work

Outcomes: Theory Development and First Empirical Tests," *Human Relations* 66, no. 2 (2013): 167–192, http://doi.org/10.1177/0018726712454554.

6. See Christine Porath, "The Leadership Behavior That's Most Important to Employees," *Harvard Business Review,* May 11, 2015, https://hbr.org/2015/05/the-leadership-behavior-thats-most-important-to-employees.

7. Anneloes Rae. "Top Team Behavior for Winning Results: Unity Starts in the C-Suite," IESE Insight, 20 (2014), 31–38. http://doi.org/10.15581/002.ART-2499.

8. See Robert Kelley, "In Praise of Followers," *Harvard Business Review,* November 1988, https://hbr.org/1988/11/in-praise-of-followers.

9. Andrew J. Ward, Melenie J. Lankau, Allen C. Amason, Jeffrey A. Sonnenfeld, and Bradley R. Agle, "Improving the Performance of Top Management Teams," *MIT Sloan Management Review,* Spring 2007, http://sloanreview.mit.edu/article/improving-the-performance-of-top-management-teams/.

10. Richard M. Rosen and Fred Adair, "CEOs Misperceive Top Teams' Performance," *Harvard Business Review* 85, no. 9 (2007): 30.

11. Thomas Oliver, *The Real Coke, the Real Story* (New York: Penguin Books, 1987).

12. Andrew J. Ward, Melenie J. Lankau, Allen C. Amason, Jeffrey A. Sonnenfeld, and Bradley R. Agle, "Improving the Performance of Top Management Teams," *MIT Sloan Management Review,* Spring 2007, http://sloanreview.mit.edu/article/improving-the-performance-of-top-management-teams/.

13. See Brooks's book, *Business Adventures,* cited earlier (note 3).

14. Rob Cross and Jon Katzenbach, "The Right Role for Top Teams, *Strategy + Business,* May 29, 2012. www.strategy-business.com/article/00103?gko=97c39.

15. Chris Smith, "Open City," *New York,* September 26, 2010, http://nymag.com/news/features/establishments/68511/.

16. Robert I. Sutton and Huggy Rao, *Scaling Up Excellence: Getting to More Without Settling for Less* (New York: Crown Publishing Group, 2014).

17. Liz Wiseman and Greg Mckeown, *Multipliers: How the Best Leaders Make Everyone Smarter* (New York: HarperBusiness, 2010).

18. David Allen, *Getting Things Done: The Art of Stress-Free Productivity*, New York: Penguin Books, 2002).

Chapter 9

1. See Michael C. Mankins's writeup of this study, published in *Harvard Business Review* on April 29, 2014, https://hbr.org/2014/04/how-a-weekly-meeting-took-up-300000-hours-a-year/.

2. As cited in "Committees that Work," a *Bain Brief* written by James Hadley and Jenny Davis-Peccoud, August 8, 2012, www.bain.com/publications/articles/decision-insights-committees-that-work.aspx.

3. Quote from page 29 of Charan and Useem's book (co-authored with Dennis Carey), *Boards That Lead: When to Take Charge, When to Partner, and When to Stay Out of the Way* (Boston: Harvard Business Review Press, 2013).

4. This anecdote was drawn from a AAA paper presented by Elizabeth Briody at the 2013 Annual Meeting of the American Anthropological Association in Chicago: "Experiencing the Resistance First Hand: Guiding Change as President of the Board of Trustees."

5. Lisa Quast, "Reverse Mentoring: What It Is and Why It Is Beneficial," *Forbes*, www.forbes.com/sites/work-in-progress/2011/01/03/reverse-mentoring-what-is-it-and-why-is-it-beneficial/.

6. See Zachary Gabriel Green and Rene J. Molenkamp, *The BART System of Group and Organizational Analysis: Boundary, Authority, Role, and Task*, https://www.it.uu.se/edu/course/homepage/projektDV/ht09/BART&uscore;Green&uscore;Molenkamp.pdf.

Conclusion

1. See "The Rise of the Sharing Economy," *The Economist*, March 9, 2013, print edition, www.economist.com/news/leaders/21573104-internet-everything-hire-rise-sharing-economy.

2. See more of the PWC scenarios on the future of work at www.pwc.com/gx/en/managing-tomorrows-people/future-of-work/journey-to-2022.jhtml.

3. For more on organizations' experience with Holacracy, see Rebecca Greenfield's article, "Holawhat? Meet the Alt-Management System Invented by a Programmer and Used by Zappos," *Fast Company*, August 1, 2015, www.fastcompany.com/3044352/the-secrets-of-holacracy.

4. This story and quote come from an article written by *Courrier Japan* in June 2013, translated by IDEO and posted on their website: www.ideo.com/images/uploads/news/pdfs/courrier&uscore;japon_news_a.pdf.

5. Jason Fried, co-founder of Basecamp (formerly known as 37signals), "Why I Run a Flat Company," *Inc.*, April 2011, www.inc.com/magazine/20110401/jason-fried-why-i-run-a-flat-company.html.

6. Statistics from the U.S. Bureau of Labor Statistics, as reported by Jeff Wald in *Forbes* magazine at www.forbes.com/sites/waldleventhal/2014/07/01/a-modern-human-capital-talent-strategy-using-freelancers/.

7. See H. Scott Matthews and Eric Williams, "Telework Adoption and Energy Use in Building and Transport Sectors in the United States and Japan," *Journal Infrastructure Systems* (American Society of Civil Engineers) 11, no. 1 (March 2005).

8. Study discussed in Erin Reid, "Why Some Men Pretend to Work 80-Hour Weeks," *Harvard Business Review*, April 28, 2015, https://hbr.org/2015/04/why-some-men-pretend-to-work-80-hour-weeks.

9. Discussed in Nicholas Bloom with James Liang, John Roberts, and Zichung Jenny Ying, "Does Working from Home Work? Evidence from a Chinese Experiment," *Quarterly Journal of Economics*, February 26, 2015, https://web.stanford.edu/~nbloom/WFH.pdf.

10. For a complete account of the making of *Birdman*, see Kirsten Acuna's article in *Business Insider*, "Here's How Ridiculously Difficult It Was to Film *Birdman* in 30 Days," October 21, 2014, www.businessinsider.com/birdman-how-it-was-filmed-2014-10.

11. From Adam Davidson's *On Money* column for the *New York Times* magazine, May 10, 2015, www.nytimes.com/2015/05/10/magazine/what-hollywood-can-teach-us-about-the-future-of-work.html.

12. Gibson has been quoted saying this at least twice on National Public Radio, including "The Science in Science Fiction," November 30, 1999. It can be found at www.npr.org/templates/story/story.php?storyId=1067220.

13. Schwaber and Sutherland have written a book on the SCRUM technique of teaming, *Scrum: The Art of Doing Twice the Work in Half the Time* (New York: Crown Business, 2014), www.forbes.com/sites/alexkonrad/2014/08/20/marc-benioffs-innovation-secret/.

14. Alex Konrad writes about Marc Benioff and the V2MOM system in "Salesforce Innovation Secrets: How Marc Benioff's Team Stays on Top," *Forbes*, August 20, 2014, www.forbes.com/sites/alexkonrad/2014/08/20/marc-benioffs-innovation-secret/.

15. From Alex Konrad's *Salesforce Innovation Secrets: How Marc Benioff's Team Stays on Top*, *Forbes* online, August 20, 2014.

RESOURCES

3×3 Framework Tools

In our experience, using a few key tools is the best way to translate concepts and frameworks into real performance outcomes for your team. Here, we provide you with three tools to help guide you through the three steps of our HPT process. The Part I chapters provide many more useful ways for you to apply the 3×3 Framework to your specific team challenges, but the tools below are the ones to get started with.

Step 1 Tool: Commitments Chartering Process

Chartering can happen in a day-long retreat, or iteratively over many quick meetings. However you choose to charter, you should make sure you are answering certain key questions that get to the heart of the three HPT foundations. Use the questions below as a checklist to ensure you are covering the most important team issues.

Goals
Have we created specific milestones?
Have we answered the WIIFM and WIIFMO questions?
Are we using If/Then thinking?

Roles
Do we have the right skills and expertise?
What informal roles do we need to establish?
(For example: advisor, facilitator, coordinator, devil's advocate)
Are roles meaningful for each person?
Have we defined our team structure and how our roles complement each other?

Norms
How will we handle conflict?
How will we communicate?
How will we make decisions?
Have we focused on just a few rules that matter?

Step 2 Tool: Misalignments Worksheet

This tool helps you get specific about potential misalignments that could be preventing your team members from following through on their commitments. The worksheet addresses group problems at the three levels of situational awareness: Interpersonal, Team and Environmental.

Instructions:

1. In the left column, list the commitments you created in the team chartering process.

2. In the center column, note specific actions and behaviors you have seen that you believe go against or ignore the commitments you made.

3. In the final column, list environmental factors that could have caused these gaps. For each conflict, ask the following questions:

   ◆ Are my team members' personal commitments outside of work causing conflicts with their team commitments?

   ◆ Are the other teams in the organization your members are a part of affecting their contribution to this team, because of looming dead-lines or other issues?

   ◆ Has there been a shift in organizational priorities that led to this conflict, such as new projects, initiatives, policies, or systems?

   ◆ Has anything changed in the market that is affecting your project, such as customer trends, new legislation, or technological developments?

Commitments	Behavior Gap	Situational Factors

Step 3 Tool: STAR Model

After identifying misalignments, use this tool to close the gap between saying and doing. The STAR model is a guide for creating actionable behavioral change. Any changes you suggest should meet the criteria listed below to maximize the likelihood they will succeed.

Be Specific

What one to three specific goals are you committing to tackle?

For example: I will spend at least three hours a month talking about strategy with people from different divisions.

Take Small Steps

Describe the small steps you're going to take toward achieving your stated goals.

For example: I will identify three individuals from different departments with whom interaction will have the biggest impact on my work.

Alter the Environment

In what ways will you alter your environment to facilitate your new goals?

For example: I will create automatically recurring meetings on my calendar so that the time is regularly blocked off and I don't have to spend additional effort scheduling each month.

Be a Realistic Optimist

Describe why you may or may not be successful in reaching your goals–specifically outline any barriers or success factors you anticipate encountering along the way.

Seven Common Mistakes Checklist

These are the pitfalls that teams tend to fall into as they set expectations and execute. Keeping an eye on the list below will help you remain vigilant about these traps.

1. Overemphasizing Abstract Goals: Align big goals with small milestones and specific personal commitments.

2. Underemphasizing Roles: It's not just about having the right people, but also putting them in the right position.

3. Undervaluing Relationships: Taking time for rapport building pays dividends in team performance.

4. Making Too Many Rules: Focus on the few key norms that will have the biggest impact for your team.

5. Ignoring Reflection: Check-ins can be as simple as a weekly stand-up meeting. The important thing is to make space for them.

6. Failing to Sell the Change: In planning any team change, create a strategy for bringing others along.

7. Putting Procedure Before Process: Treat the 3×3 framework as an ongoing conversation, not as a box to check once before moving on.

1. Overemphasizing Abstract Goals
2. Underemphasizing Roles
3. Undervaluing Relationships
4. Making Too Many Rules
5. Not Checking In Enough
6. Celebrating the "Great Man"
7. Putting Procedure before Process

Team Cultural Archetypes Assessment

Mark each statement about your team below as follows:

0 = Rarely true for my team

1 = Sometimes true for my team

2 = Equally true and not true for my team

3 = Usually true for my team

4 = Always true for my team

____A. The team leader defines roles and tasks.

____D. When working, team members tend to keep to themselves.

____C. Team members tend to make decisions as a group.

____B. Team members tend to work collaboratively on tasks.

____A. The team leader sets the direction and others follow.

_____C. Team members are generally free to pick the tasks they want to work on.

_____D. Team members focus on what they do well and they get it done right.

_____B. Team members frequently seek out one another's input on their work.

_____D. Team members often have significant disagreements over direction, but they keep their opinions to themselves.

_____A. Decision-making follows a strict chain of command.

_____B. We are usually on the same page.

_____C. The best idea wins, no matter whom it came from.

_____D. The team moves forward on a decision even if some do not agree with it.

_____A. When team members disagree, the person with the most authority decides what to do.

_____C. The chain of command exists more on paper than in practice.

_____B. The team generally does not move forward on a decision until everyone is on board with it.

_____A. Everyone knows his or her role and sticks to it.

_____D. It is not important that team members see eye to eye.

_____C. Team members manage themselves with little direction from the leader.

_____B. When making decisions, team members avoid ruffling one another's feathers.

Add Up Your Scores

Now add up the total of the numbers next to each letter. Your total scores for letters A through D should fall between 0 and 20.

A (MORE HIERARCHICAL) = _____

C (MORE FLAT) = _____

and

B (MORE COHESIVE) = _____

$\boldsymbol{D}$ (MORE INDIVIDUALISTIC) = _____

Subtract $\boldsymbol{C}$ from A (this may be a negative number): $A - \boldsymbol{C} =$ _____

This is your score on the **vertical** axis of the team culture grid.

Subtract $\boldsymbol{D}$ from B (this may be a negative number): $B - \boldsymbol{D} =$ _____

This is your score on the **horizontal** axis of the team culture grid.

Plot the point on the grid (where these two scores meet). This is your team culture type.

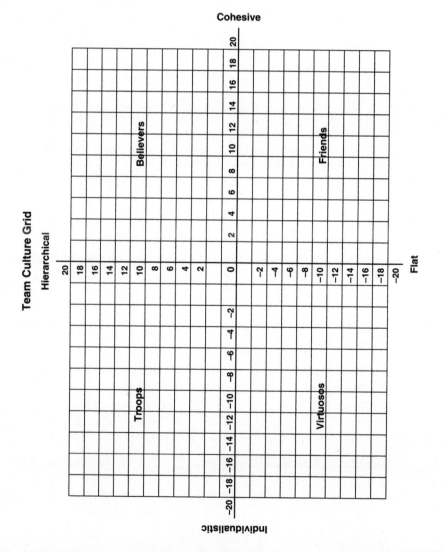

BIBLIOGRAPHY

Anthropological, Sociological, and Other Academic Works

Becker, Howard S. *Outsiders: Studies in the Sociology of Deviance*. New York: The Free Press, 1963.

Geertz, Clifford. *The Interpretation of Cultures; Selected Essays*. New York: Basic Books, 1973.

Mauss, Marcel. *The Gift: Forms and Functions of Exchange in Archaic Societies*. New York: W.W. Norton & Company, 2000.

Rappaport, Harold A. *Pigs for the Ancestors: Ritual in the Ecology of a New Guinea People*. Long Grove, IL: Waveland Press, 2000.

Business Books, Biographies, and Industry Studies

Boyd, Drew, and Jacob Goldenberg. *Inside the Box: A Proven System of Creativity for Breakthrough Results*. New York: Simon & Schuster, 2014.

Briody, Elizabeth K. "Experiencing the Resistance First Hand: Guiding Change as President of the Board of Trustees." Presented at the Annual Meeting of the American Anthropological Association. Chicago, 2013.

Briody, Elizabeth K, Robert T. Trotter, and Tracy L. Meerwarth. *Transforming Culture: Creating and Sustaining a Better Manufacturing Organization*. New York: Palgrave Macmillan, 2010.

Brooks, John. *Business Adventures: Twelve Classic Tales from the World of Wall Street*. New York: Open Road Integrated Media, 2014.

Charan, Ram, et al. *Boards That Lead: When to Take Charge, When to Partner, and When to Stay Out of the Way*. Boston: Harvard Business School Publishing, 2014.

Collins, Jim, and Morten T. Hansen. *Great by Choice: Uncertainty, Chaos, and Luck—Why Some Thrive Despite Them All*. New York: HarperCollins, 2011.

Fried, Jason, and David Heinemeier Hansson. *Remote: Office Not Required*. New York: Crown Publishing Group, 2013.

Grant, Adam M. *Give and Take: Why Helping Others Drives Our Success*. New York: Penguin Books, 2011.

Hansen, Morten. *Collaboration: How Leaders Avoid the Traps, Build Common Ground, and Reap Big Results*. Boston: Harvard Business Review Press, 2009.

Livingston, Jessica. *Founders at Work: Stories of Startups' Early Days*. Berkeley, CA: Apress, 2009.

Marcinko, Richard. *Rogue Warrior*. New York: Simon & Schuster, 2009.

McChrystal, General Stanley, et al. *Team of Teams: New Rules of Engagement for a Complex World*. New York: Portfolio, 2015.

Oliver, Thomas. *The Real Coke, the Real Story*. New York: Penguin Books, 1987.

Ries, Eric. *The Lean Startup: How Today's Entrepreneurs Use Continuous Innovation to Create Radically Successful Businesses*. New York: Crown Business, 2011.

Schwaber, Ken, and Jeff Sutherland. *Scrum: The Art of Doing Twice the Work in Half the Time*. New York: Crown Business, 2014.

Schwarz, Roger M. *The Skilled Facilitator: A Comprehensive Resource for Consultants, Facilitators, Managers, Trainers, and Coaches*. 2nd edition. San Francisco: Jossey-Bass, 2002.

Sutton, Robert I., and Huggy Rao. *Scaling Up Excellence: Getting to More Without Settling for Less*. New York: Crown Publishing Group, 2014.

Terwiesch, Christian, and Karl Ulrich. *Innovation Tournaments: Creating and Selecting Exceptional Opportunities*. Boston: Harvard Business Review Press, 2009.

Thaler, Richard H., and Cass R. Sunstein. *Nudge: Improving Decisions About Health, Wealth, and Happiness*. New York: Penguin Group, 2008.

Vogelstein, Fred. *Dogfight: How Apple and Google Went to War and Started a Revolution*. New York: Sarah Crichton Books, 2013.

Wiseman, Liz, and Greg Mckeown. *Multipliers: How the Best Leaders Make Everyone Smarter*. New York: HarperBusiness, 2010.

Teamwork and Dynamics

Boynton, Andy, and Bill Fischer. *Virtuoso Teams: Lessons from Teams that Changed Their Worlds*. London: Financial Times–Prentice Hall, 2005.

Edmondson, Amy C. *Teaming: How Organizations Learn, Innovate, and Compete in the Knowledge Economy*. San Francisco: Jossey-Bass, 2012.

Gawande, Atul. *The Checklist Manifesto: How to Get Things Right*. New York: Metropolitan Books, 2009.

Hackman, J. Richard. *Leading Teams: Setting the Stage for Great Performances*. Boston: Harvard Business School Publishing Corporation, 2002.

Thompson, Leigh. *Creative Conspiracy: The New Rules of Breakthrough Collaboration*. Boston: Harvard Business Review Press, 2013.

Personal Psychology and Personal Effectiveness

Allen, David. *Getting Things Done: The Art of Stress-Free Productivity*. New York: The Penguin Group, 2001.

Arnold, Caroline L. *Small Move, Big Change: Using Microresolutions to Transform Your Life Permanently*. New York: Penguin Group, 2014.

Bloom, Jeremy. *Fueled By Failure: Using Detours and Defeats to Power Progress*. Irvine, CA: Entrepreneur Press, 2015.

Cain, Susan. *Quiet: The Power of Introverts in a World that Can't Stop Talking*. New York: Broadway Books, 2013.

Covey, Stephen. *The 7 Habits of Highly Effective People: Powerful Lessons of Personal Change*. New York: Simon & Schuster, 1989.

Duhigg, Charles. *The Power of Habit: Why We Do What We Do in Life and Business*. New York: Random House, 2014.

Epley, Nicholas. *Mindwise: Why We Misunderstand What Others Think, Believe, Feel, and Want*. New York: Vintage Books, 2014.

Halvorson, Heidi Grant. *Nine Things Successful People Do Differently*. Boston: Harvard Business Review Press, 2011.

Johnson, Steve. *Where Good Ideas Come from*. New York: Riverhead Books, 2011.

Kahneman, Daniel. *Thinking, Fast and Slow*. New York: Farrar, Straus and Giroux, 2013.

Kohlrieser, George, Susan Goldsworthy, and Duncan Coombe. *Care to Dare: Unleashing Astonishing Potential Through Secure Base Leadership*. San Francisco: Jossey-Bass, 2012.

McClusky, Mark. *Faster, Higher, Stronger: How Sports Science Is Creating a New Generation of Superathletes—and What We Can Learn from Them*. New York: Hudson Street Press, 2014.

Nussbaum, Bruce. *Creative Intelligence: Harnessing the Power to Create, Connect, and Inspire*. New York: HarperBusiness, 2013.

Shell, G. Richard, and Mario Moussa. *The Art of Woo: Using Strategic Persuasion to Sell Your Ideas*. New York: The Penguin Group, 2008.

Shell, G. Richard. *Bargaining for Advantage: Negotiation Strategies for Reasonable People*. New York: Penguin Books, 2000.

History and Popular Culture

Apatow, Judd. *Sick in the Head: Conversations about Life and Comedy*. New York: Random House, 2015.

Bonsall, Thomas. *Disaster in Dearborn: The Story of the Edsel*. Redwood City, CA: Stanford University Press, 2002.

Hodges, Andrew, and Douglas Hofstadter. *Alan Turing: The Enigma: The Book That Inspired the Film The Imitation Game*. Princeton, NJ: Princeton University Press, 2014.

Krakauer, Jon. *Into Thin Air: A Personal Account of the Mt. Everest Disaster*. Princeton, NJ: Anchor Books, 1999.

Martin, Steve. *Born Standing Up: A Comic's Life*. New York: Scribner, 2007.

McDougall, Walter A. *The Heavens and the Earth: A Political History of the Space Age*. Baltimore: Johns Hopkins University Press, 1985.

McNamee, Thomas. *Alice Waters and Chez Panisse* New York: Penguin Books, 2008.

Morsey, Chase, Jr. *The Man Who Saved the V-8: The Untold Stories of Some of the Most Important Product Decisions in the History of Ford Motor Company*. North Charleston, SC: CreateSpace Independent Publishing Platform, 2014.

Richards, Keith, and James Fox. *Life*. New York: Back Bay Books, 2011.

Sinclair, Upton. *I, Candidate for Governor: And How I Got Licked*. Oakland: University of California Press, 1935 (1994).

THE AUTHORS

Mario Moussa, PhD, teaches in EDP and oversees the HPT observer team. He is the co-director of the Wharton Strategic Persuasion Workshop and the co-author (with G. Richard Shell) of *The Art of Woo: Using Strategic Persuasion to Sell Your Ideas*. As a management consultant, Mario advises leaders at the world's top companies about organizational effectiveness, strategy, and change.

Madeleine Boyer is a doctoral candidate in anthropology at the University of Pennsylvania. She is a lecturer at the Wharton School. She is also a business anthropologist who consults for Fortune 500 companies on teamwork, collaboration, and managing organizational culture.

Derek Newberry, PhD, is a business anthropologist specializing in the human factors that drive organizational effectiveness. He is a lecturer at the Wharton School and teaches in the Wharton Executive Education program. He also consults for Fortune 500 companies and leading nonprofits on enhancing collaboration and managing organizational culture.

Contributing Authors

Joanne Baron, PhD, is a lecturer in the department of anthropology at the University of Pennsylvania. Since 2013, she has worked in EDP, where she has been an observer and also taken the role of foreign government. She has also worked on developing the EDP simulation, adding cultural challenges for participants to overcome.

Vishal Bhatia specializes in people and culture development. A former director at the Wharton School, he deepened connectivity and experiential learning among students. He is the founder of OfficialCOMMUNITY, a music management firm that represents iconic artists and pioneered the industry-changing concept of developing and monetizing online fan-communities. He also has background in sports, television, child development, government and paramilitary.

Amy Brown, PhD, is a social anthropologist and educator who draws on years of experience as a qualitative researcher, teacher, curriculum writer, and professional developer to help teams and individuals maximize their potential. Her book, *A Good Investment? Philanthropy and the Marketing of Race in an Urban Public School*, was published by the University of Minnesota Press. She is a faculty member in the Critical Writing Program at the University of Pennsylvania.

Lauren Hirshon is an organizational change and transformation consultant for governments, nonprofits, and businesses. She is currently the director of operations and development for an applied research and advisory program at Harvard and a lecturer at the Wharton School.

Michael Joiner's research and work in global health over the past 20 years have taken him to some of the most remote and programmatically challenging environments on Earth. He is based in Philadelphia and Paris and holds a PhD in medical anthropology from the University of Pennsylvania.

Annette Mattei is an independent consultant who supports governmental and nonprofit organizations in developing and executing research initiatives and other mission-related activities.

Renée Gillespie Torchia, PhD, is an anthropologist who helps leaders understand how personality, communication, and culture influence business outcomes. Renée has coached individuals and teams in Wharton Executive Education and ran a change management consulting practice for companies of excellence. She is now vice president of talent strategy and culture for an international data analytics and risk assessment company in New York City.

INDEX